Loosening the Knot of Oppression

Robert Mackay

Loosening the Knot of Oppression
Robert Mackay

Copyright © 2024 by Ocean Droplets - www.oceandroplets.com

All rights reserved. No portion of this book may be reproduced in any form without the prior written consent of the publisher or a license from The Canadian Copyright Licensing Agency (www.accesscopyright.ca).

ISBN 978-1-7781313-4-9 (print)

Every reasonable effort has been made to acquire permissions to reproduce copyrighted materials used in this text.

For those who know they are oppressed,

and those who may not realize it.

Table of Contents

Preface vii
The Knot 1
The Pyramid 5
    Our nature 8
        Cooperation 8
        Competition 10
        Care and Control 11
    A long tradition 12
    Inequality 15
    Keeping it together 18
    The devastating effects 22
    Response to pressure 25
The Globe 29
    A Divine Messenger 31
    Reaction and Result 33
    A New Social Model 36
The Báb 41
    Transforming the Hearts 45
Bahá'u'lláh 51
    The Revelation 54
    The Book of Certitude 56

    The Proclamation 60
    The Most Great Prison 64
    The Most Holy Book 66
    Final Triumph 67
The Covenant 73
    Spiritual Beings 76
    'Abdu'l-Bahá—The Center 79
    Shoghi Effendi—The Builder 86
    The Learned and the Rulers 91
    Separation of Function 94
Personal Transformation 99
    Purifying the heart 101
    Making better choices 103
    Tests 105
    Taking responsibility 107
    Service 110
Social Development 115
    Creating Unity 116
    Authority 118
    Consultation 122
    Obedience 126
Paradigm Shift 131
    Features of a paradigm shift 132
    A New Social Paradigm 135
    Guidance and Vision 137
Getting Started 143
    Recognize 143

- Where is God? 145
- Reset 148
  - Choice Wine 149
  - Enemies to Friends 150
- Reflect 153
- Reach Out 157
- References 163

Preface

This book is one outcome of a nine-year sojourn in Thailand and Chile in the 1990s. Living outside my native North American culture, I noticed certain aspects of society in each of these countries that seemed strangely dysfunctional. Something was not quite right, but I could not put my finger on it.

Then, towards the end of this period, I happened to read *Uncle Tom's Cabin* by Harriet Beecher Stowe. Two overlapping ideas came to me. First, the behavior of people in Chile and Thailand that I could not understand was likely rooted in a history of oppression. And second, my own country had its own tragic history of oppression—probably far worse than either of them. Stepping out of my box and peering into other realities helped shine a light on certain truths of my own heritage that I may have otherwise never noticed. In some ways, I was the oppressor; in some ways I was the oppressed.

This understanding of the problem gave me a greater appreciation of a new vision of the world I had recently encountered. It occurred to me that answers I had discovered in my personal search might touch others in some way. What follows is my attempt to share them.

The Knot

"Justice is, in this day, bewailing its plight, and Equity groaneth beneath the yoke of oppression. The thick clouds of tyranny have darkened the face of the earth, and enveloped its peoples."[1] - Bahá'u'lláh

Oppression. What a drag. I don't want to talk about it. The very word brings up images of slavery, dictatorships, forced labor camps, caste systems, colonialism, and genocide. What a waste of human life and talent. Why bother thinking about it? It's better just to ignore it, forget about it, change the topic.

I wish we could. But unfortunately thousands of years of oppression have had a deep effect on us and our civilization. You can hardly find a single country today that isn't suffering from some serious problem, be it ethnic conflicts, political corruption, civil strife, or economic collapse. Our global society is sick. Just look at the high rates of depression, divorce, wife and child abuse, drug addiction, alcoholism, and crime in every land. Time-honored institutions like the church, the state, big business and the family seem to be losing their relevance and cohesive power. All these symptoms trace back to a common disease: oppression.

Conventional wisdom says you can't fight back. The problems are too big and the system will never change. You might as well just try to stay out of trouble, do the best you can, keep your job, save a little money, hope your kids turn out OK, and be the best person you can be.

I wish it were that simple. Unfortunately, these problems are starting to intrude into our "safe" lives. They touch each of us. When a troubled soul goes on a killing spree, we fear for friends and our children. When a country launches a war, it affects the world economy. An irrational decision by a single millionaire can throw hundreds of employees out of work. People around us are stressed out, lonely, angry or depressed. They are feeling pain. So are we.

Why? How did things get this way? Wasn't life simpler once? Is it our destiny as a race to suffer so much? Certainly it is our history. Looking back over the past many centuries, we see a lot of suffering—slavery, feudalism, colonialism, and exploitation carried out by tyrants, despots and dictators— and always war after war. It's obvious that a key element in our history, our civilization, and our culture, is oppression. Although oppression once permitted a relative degree of human progress, it has now become a knot in the rope of civilization. It's blocking our growth. What's more, it's weakening the very fibers of the rope itself, threatening to break it. If the rope of civilization breaks, we will all lose. In fact, although we may not feel oppressed, nor see ourselves as oppressors, it is virtually impossible to escape from the effects of oppression. It is the urgent task of every one of us who cares to do what we can to remove this knot. The question is, how?

In the past, people have responded to oppression in two ways—comply or resist. They either ignored the knot, and tried to get along as best they could, or they fought against it. But neither of these responses solves the problem. Compliance soon turns into cooperation, making the knot bigger. But resistance doesn't solve the problem either. Resisting tightens the knot, because you cannot remove a knot from a rope by pulling on it; that only makes it tighter. Our history books are filled with people who complied and people who resisted, but the knot of oppression remains to this day.

This book presents a different solution. It too has been used in the past, but its power and effectiveness have become misunderstood, diluted, and lost over time. The solution takes us beyond the push-and-pull arena of the competitive, material world, and opens us to a small corner of reality we often overlook—the human heart. The way to loosen the knot of oppression can be found in our hearts, where love resides. We must fill our hearts with love, a powerful love, an invincible and divine love that can come only from our Creator. When we find this love and fill our hearts with it, we will have the power we need to loosen the knot of oppression.

When and how did this solution work in the past? Why did it stop working? How can we use it today? These are some of the questions this book addresses. But before we look at the solution, we need to share an understanding of what oppression is, how it works, and what are its strengths and weaknesses. After that we'll look at how it was overcome in the past, and why the solution at that time was only partial. Then, in the main part of the book we'll consider a more recent, more complete, and more effective means of loosening the knot of oppression than ever witnessed in the history of mankind.

Notes

1. Bahá'u'lláh, *Tablets of Bahá'u'lláh*, p 84

The Pyramid

Welcome to the pyramid. It stands tall and proud, a monument to civilization, enormous at its base, rising step by step, level by level, higher and higher to a point. Look closely and you will see it is made up of blocks—rows upon rows of blocks. Each block is hard and square. They fit together perfectly. The blocks in the bottom level support those in the next level up. That level supports the next and so on up to the top. At the top there is just one block. The next level down has four. The next has nine and so on. In a pyramid with, say, 10 levels you'll find 385 blocks. It's compact. It's well organized. It's hierarchical. It's a model for social organization.

Governments follow this model. At the top you have the king, prime minister, or president. Under him the ministers and members of cabinets and congresses. Below them are various officials, aides, and diplomats. Then come the bureaucrats—office workers, civil servants, police officers, and postal clerks.

Businesses also follow this model, with the president at the top; then the vice presidents, division managers and their assistants; then department heads and supervisors; and finally, the employees, who are often ranked hierarchically as well. And this isn't just big businesses. Restaurants, for example, have well-defined hierarchies of managers, cooks, waiters, busboys, and dishwashers.

The military adheres strictly to the pyramid model. From top down it goes from commander-in-chief to generals, majors, captains, and lieutenants, and then on down through various levels of sergeants and common soldiers.

Religious organizations are commonly based on this model as well. At the top you find the Pope, the Dalai Lama or the Ayatollah. Then you have the bishops, high priests, or learned mullás. Below them, in various types of hierarchies, you find the rest of the clergy. Finally, at the bottom, are the common believers.

Most other social organizations have some kind of pyramid-shaped hierarchy too. Schools generally have hierarchies in administration and among the teaching staff, as well as among the students. Clubs tend to have presidents, senior and junior officers, and voting members. Sports teams have their captains, starting players, and bench-sitters. Even the Boy Scouts are ranked top to bottom from Eagle to Tenderfoot.

Finally, looking at the basic unit of social organization, we see that the family is often organized hierarchically by age and generation, with the parents at the top, then the children (in order by age), and finally the grandchildren.

The pyramid is everywhere, and it seems to be the most successful way to organize our society. In fact, it's hard to imagine any other form of social organization. The pyramid is efficient, positioning the most capable people at the top. It's said to be natural because it follows human nature and it mirrors certain hierarchies we find in the animal kingdom. It has stood the test of time. Human society has followed this model for thousands of years. Many believe that our civilization could not have advanced as far as it has without this type of organization. Yes, it looks like the pyramid model for human society is here to stay.

Unfortunately, though, the pyramid has a weakness—oppression. It is oppressive because it is built on the principle of domination. The mere act of stacking blocks one on top of another introduces a need for force, domination, and control, because nobody wants to be at the bottom. And it is a basic law of the pyramid that for every block on top, many more must be below. The majestic height of the tower of blocks obscures the fact that the unlucky ones at the bottom bear the weight.

Since the pyramid is a basic pattern of our civilization, we can expect to find domination and oppression as integral parts of our society. Looking around we see that to be true. The strong dominate the weak. Men dominate women. The clever and skillful take advantage of the clumsy and ignorant. It's white over black, rich over poor, upper class over lower class, educated over illiterate, and the young, strong and beautiful over the old, weak and ugly.

Our nature

How did we get this way? How did this pyramid ever come to be? Is it really our nature to compete, to dominate, and to oppress? Is this really a dog-eat-dog world where only the fittest survive?

Possibly not. Or maybe the "fittest" isn't what we might think. In a new book, *Survival of the Friendliest*, authors Brian Hare and Vanessa Woods explore the question of what makes a species fit to survive. Their historical and laboratory research indicates that several species, including Homo sapiens, came out on top not by being stronger or more cruel, but instead by being friendly and cooperating with each other. The fittest for survival turn out to be the friendliest ones. In fact, Charles Darwin himself observed this trend among the species he studied. He wrote, "those communities, which included the greatest number of the most sympathetic members, would flourish best and rear the greatest number of offspring."

Cooperation

Our innate ability to cooperate is confirmed in another recent book, *The Dawn of Everything: A New History of Humanity*, by David Graeber and David Wengrow. It provides exhaustive details of archeological discoveries over the last few decades that are shedding new light on our distant and recent past. Excavations on sites in modern-day Turkey, Ukraine, China, Peru, and the United States, among others, have uncovered evidence that the people in some large pre-historic communities shared the wealth and enjoyed relatively equal social status. The remains of their houses are all about the same size, with no trace of palaces, monuments, or mansions. Artifacts recovered from their tombs and homes suggest roughly equal amounts of material possessions.

Sites currently under excavation suggest that there was a variety of approaches to social organization across the continents for many centuries. Most groups sustained themselves by hunting game and gathering food, both of which were abundant in the fertile floodplains where major civilizations developed. These groups grew to number in the thousands, often without the need of sustained agriculture, and in many cases they were able to manage themselves with little or no hierarchy. There is every indication that they organized and governed themselves through consultative assemblies and councils. They often developed safeguards to ensure relatively stable, egalitarian civilizations that lasted for hundreds of years. This kind of non-oppressive governance continued among certain indigenous groups in the Americas into present times, and was recorded by various European explorers upon their first contact with them.

Competition

Of course, not every society evolved along these lines. There were also groups that favored more hierarchical relationships. Often located in areas where food was less abundant and physical prowess was more valued, people in these groups may have come to follow strong individuals who could command respect and lead decisively. At the same time, they may have viewed the more cooperative societies with contempt—and the feeling may have been mutual.

In fact, there is ample evidence that pre-historic peoples grouped themselves into "culture areas" with similar ways of gathering and processing food, observing religious rites, or organizing themselves socially and politically. Such distinctions can create a sense of belonging and identity within the group, but can also lead to feelings of superiority among members towards the people in other groups.

This tendency of people to separate themselves into "us" and "them" groups stems from our survival instincts, according to Hare and Woods. Part of being friendly means protecting each other from any perceived threat, including outsiders, as a mother bear protects her cubs. They observe that friendly, self-protecting groups can be formed under virtually any criteria, such as classmates, fans of a sports team, street gangs, or international service club members. We humans have a unique ability to identify with anyone in our group, along with an equally powerful tendency to exclude, despise, de-humanize and even attack those who are not.

Sadly, it seems that from the Stone Age to modern times, human nature has not changed very much. Without some kind of moral compass, people may descend a slippery slope from looking down on other groups, to de-humanizing them, to justifying violence against them, and finally, starting wars and taking slaves. Anyone who wonders why or how a skillful politician can pit one group of people against another will find some well-reasoned answers in the research of Hare and Woods.

Care and Control

Pursuing another line of inquiry into human nature, Graeber and Wengrow mention a care/violence relationship that may stem from a more general care/control duality. For example, at the intimate level of the family, unfavorable conditions may turn genuine care between spouses into jealousy, fear of separation, and a desire to control. Likewise, a parent who cares deeply for a child must guard against excessive worry or attachment that can lead to oppressive domination.

At the organized level of an institution, be it a school, church, municipal office or humanitarian aid agency, how many sincere teachers, pastors, civil servants, or field-workers may have at some time or other reached a point of frustration in dealing with "these unruly kids", "these stubborn parishioners", "these annoying complainers", or "these ungrateful recipients" and felt the urge to do something stern or even violent in an effort to control the situation? And those are the nice people. What about the ones with less pure motives that hold such positions?

Clearly, our humanity includes the potential to do good or do harm. Our friendly, caring nature can degrade into a fearful or dominating one. Individually, we may have some freedom to choose our behavior. But in a society, we live with the consequences of other people's choices. How might such choices from the distant past have brought us to the pyramid we find ourselves stuck in today?

A long tradition

Somehow, despite the variety of social models that humanity may have started with, we are now left with just one: an oppresive hierarchical pyramid. Graeber and Wengrow offer an explanation of how that could have come about. They suggest that the seeds of inequality come from slight differences in social status, typically gained through physical force, personal charisma, or access to esoteric knowledge. If you think about it, this seems reasonable. After all, each of us is different. Nobody is truly equal to anyone else. In any given group, some are naturally stronger, or have more personality, or are maybe more clever than others. Someone with an inflated ego in such a position might easily convince themselves and others around them that they are superior, more worthy, elite. Thus, inequality could be fertile soil for the eventual development of chiefs, politicians, or priests.

Graeber and Wengrow also point to archeological evidence in Mesopotamia and elsewhere of institutions created for the care and supervision of widows, orphans, outcasts, and captured warriors. Often an institution like this would gain the patronage of a strong, clever, or charismatic leader. Over the course of years or generations this leader and his or her family and descendants could nurture the group of dependents to become a personal retinue of loyal admirers who might feel obliged to serve them. Some of the most capable and loyal servants might be chosen to form a private police force to enforce the whims or laws of what has effectively become the ruling class.

Such, it seems, may well have been the origins of hierarchy and the pyramid of oppression. In any case, by the time history was being recorded, we find the early civilizations of Babylon, Egypt, Persia, and Greece all organized their societies hierarchically. Honor, glory, and riches went to the strong, educated, wealthy elite. Women were regarded as inferior to men. Citizens were superior to slaves—those pyramid builders of antiquity and modern times who were always in such great demand, for as pyramids aspire to grow ever higher, there's a constant need for bottom blocks.

By the time of the Roman Empire, the pattern of leadership and dominant behavior was well entrenched into habits, language, and law. Most wealthy and middle-class Roman citizens owned slaves to help with household chores. The Latin word "domus" for household can be found in our word "domestic," but also "dominion" and "dominate." Guidelines for the treatment of slaves evolved into concepts of private property and freedom, which become codified in Roman law, pervading most of Europe.

European society in the Middle Ages continued the oppressive model with its feudal system. The king was at the top, with all his ministers, lords, ladies, dukes, counts and the rest of the court below him. Then came a level of professionals—craftsmen, carpenters, bakers, blacksmiths, and weavers. Below them were the common peasants, who, though landless, worked the fields, grew the crops, and fed the nation, while barely subsisting on a small return from their labor.

Europe's love of exploration and exploitation did much to spread the ever-developing oppressive system around the world. Its kings were urged on in their mission by Pope Nicolas V, who in 1452 gave them "full and free permission to invade, search out, capture, and subjugate the Saracens [Arabs] and pagans and any other unbelievers and enemies of Christ wherever they may be ... and to reduce their persons into perpetual servitude."

By now the Europeans were quite adept at domination, conquering with cruel tactics, superior weapons, and unfamiliar diseases. Intense competition broke out among them to see which country could most effectively exploit resources, subdue and enslave native peoples, and develop the biggest markets for trade.

The countries they encountered were not total strangers to pyramid-style social orders, nor to oppression. The Aztecs and Mayas in South America had developed an elaborate social hierarchy. Tribal groups in Africa had been capturing, using, and selling each other's members as slaves for hundreds of years. Emperors in China and Japan were well acquainted with the ways and means of seizing power and controlling nations and armies. But directly or indirectly, the European colonial system has left a lasting imprint of oppression on almost every part of the world.

Inequality

Western Europeans and their offspring in North America took the initiative to move, explore, and dominate, thus setting up a pyramid-style hierarchy unequaled by anything in history, in which the wealth of the world flows to and is largely consumed by a relatively small percentage of its population. According to 2021 statistics from Credit Suisse, just over 1% of the world's population holds over 45% of its wealth, while 55% of the people have to get by on a mere 1.3% of the total. The top 10 countries in the world hold over 75% of the wealth, where just two of them by themselves (USA and China) account for almost 50% of it.

Thus we find that we can apply our pyramid model not only to individuals, but to countries. Each country is one block in the world pyramid, with the corresponding forms of oppression and inequality. Further, within each country, we again find a pyramid of oppression, each with a small group of people controlling the wealth and lives of the majority of the people in that country. And as we have seen, every aspect of society—government and the military, business, religion, education, and the family generally follow the pyramid model —where a relatively small group of people gains certain advantages by dominating the rest.

In fact, if we look more closely at our four-sided pyramid made up of regularly shaped blocks, we will discover just how unequal it is. You might think that a position half-way up, in the middle level, would be average—not on the top, but not on the bottom. A decent position. That's where you might find, say, the "middle class" in society. But how many people have that chance? It's actually a relatively privileged position.

For example, in our pyramid of 10 levels, there are 100 blocks on the lowest level, 81 blocks on the second level, 64 blocks on the third level, and so on up to the top. In all there are 385 blocks. Now let's cut it in half, right across the middle. There are five levels on top and five on the bottom.

The five levels on top contain 55 blocks (1+4+9+16+25=55).

The five levels on the bottom contain 330 blocks (36+49+64+81+100=330)

According to this calculation, out of the 385 blocks, only 55 are in the top half. The bottom half contains 330. That means that less than 15% of the blocks in the pyramid are in a "better-than-average" position. 85% of the blocks are below the half-way point, in a "worse-than-average" situation. Not only are some blocks much better off than others, the ones on top are far fewer than the ones on the bottom.

This inequality in the pyramid model shows up time and again in our society. In 2018 the World Bank reported that 3.4 billion people, close to half the world's population, were struggling to meet basic needs. A life-style considered average middle class in the West, that includes good food and clothes, adequate health care, a comfortable house, a car, and good education for the children is beyond the reach of the majority of the people of the world. That middle-class lifestyle (or better) is accessible only to those 15% living in the top half of the pyramid.

Given this inequality, given the fact that no block enjoys having another block on top of it, that no one willingly chooses to be dominated or oppressed, how, then did the pyramid ever get built in the first place? What keeps it together? Why doesn't it just fall apart? Why do those bottom blocks participate at all?

Keeping it together

Although it looks very simple and strong—formidable to say the least—it actually takes a lot of work just to keep the pyramid together. From the day that one block climbed on top of another, it had to use force to keep the bottom block down. Initially the force was brute muscular strength. Males dominated females, and the strongest males fought each other for domination of the group. We still see this type of force manifested today in contact sports, boxing, fistfights, child-beating, wife-battering, and rape.

Force is amplified with weapons: simple ones like clubs, whips, knives, swords, spears, ropes, chains, poison, and fire; and increasingly complex ones like bows and arrows, catapults, torture machines, guns, cannons, bombs, tanks, gas, airplanes, missiles, land mines, nuclear arms, and now chemical and biological weapons. These are just a few of the tools used to control the blocks and maintain the pyramid.

But weapons of force, however powerful, are limited. If used to an extreme, they will destroy the blocks, and the pyramid cannot be built. Something more powerful and less physically damaging is also necessary. What's needed is internal control—mental and psychological control.

The most basic tool of mental control is deceit. A bottom block that doesn't know it's on the bottom, or doesn't believe it, or thinks that the bottom is a great place, or that its destiny is to be there, doesn't need force to control it. All around us we see the manifestations of mental control: from the obvious ones like outright lies, propaganda programs, censorship, advertising and media control; to the less obvious such as controlled school curricula, corporate public information campaigns, social media, and the confusing smokescreen of political speeches; to the dark and sinister ones like backbiting, treachery, and betrayal.

Using these two tools of force and deceit, the top blocks can take the next step in strengthening their position, which is to gain effective control of resources. In the past this meant ownership of land and livestock. More recently it has come to include control of money, capital and natural resources, as well as the means of production and communication. Control of these resources provides a life of comfort and ease for the top blocks, and also gives them the means to reinforce and expand their control over the lower blocks in the pyramid.

Armed with tools and resources, the top blocks seem to be well in command of the situation, fully capable of maintaining the simple pyramid structure. But as the pyramid grows in size and complexity, their job gets more difficult. They need help. So they look to the middle blocks of the pyramid. These middle blocks provide a form of insulation for them— protecting them from the bottom blocks who naturally aspire to move to the top. The top blocks take advantage of this situation and develop it further. They train the middle blocks to become guards.

Howard Zinn, in his book *A People's History of the United States*, comments on this role of the middle class. He says that in a society as developed as ours has become, those in power rely on the loyalty and obedience of people who accept small tokens and rewards to keep things running. He includes police and soldiers, but also educators, clergy, bureaucrats, factory workers, and professionals like lawyers and doctors, as well as truck drivers, postal clerks, firefighters, and other municipal workers. He sees the employed middle class acting as buffers between the elite and the downtrodden.

The middle blocks are allowed certain privileges in exchange for carrying out certain duties. Looking at it from one point of view, it almost seems that all these duties serve one basic purpose: to maintain the order and stability of the pyramid. Middle blocks write and enforce laws to keep all the blocks in their proper place. They operate factories and create businesses to exploit and develop natural resources, and keep the flow of goods and services moving towards the top. They educate themselves and the lower blocks to conform to and uphold the pyramid structure. They throw down a few crumbs and entertain the bottom blocks to keep their minds off their condition.

But lest the middle blocks get too comfortable or too powerful, the top blocks have developed a way to control them as well as the bottom blocks. They use the time-tested method of divide and conquer. They set one block against the other. They initiate competition that hardens the sides of the blocks, making them more resistant to each other and to the pressure of domination that they constantly live under.

The pyramid, by its very nature, encourages competition. Each block aspires to move up. And this can only be done by bringing another block down. There's only so much room at the top, you know. The top blocks encourage this competition. Do well in school and you'll get ahead. Work hard and you'll move up. Complain about the "system" and you lose opportunities. Try to change it and down you go, straight to the bottom of the pyramid.

Where there is no natural competition, the top blocks invent it by introducing false divisions. Whites are pitted against blacks, who are set against Latinos and Asians. Long-time residents of a country are set against immigrants. Companies set up competitions between divisions. Football clubs compete for the yearly trophy. Neighbors compete for the bigger house, the nicer car, and the greenest lawn. Teenage girls, pushed by a falsely fabricated sense of inadequacy, kill themselves for the thinnest waistline, the smoothest complexion, the coolest boyfriend.

Malcolm X once talked about two kinds of slaves: house slaves and field slaves. The house slaves worked in the house doing relatively easy work. They lived in the attic or basement, wore the master's clothes, ate the master's food, and spoke with good diction like the master. They loved the master. If the master got sick, they prayed for him; if the house caught on fire, they would run for water to put it out. The field slaves, on the other hand, worked long hours in the hot sun, lived in crude huts, ate poor food, and were constantly threatened by the whip. They hated the master: if he got sick, they prayed he would die; if the house caught on fire, they hoped the wind would pick up.

The master used this artificial division to control all the slaves. Each group disapproved of the other. The field slaves resented the special treatment of the house slaves, yet some of them aspired to that position. The house slaves often thought of themselves as superior, and looked down on the field slaves. The two groups spent so much time competing against each other they often forgot that they were all the victims of a manipulative system.

All this competition brings pressure, of course. The blocks in the pyramid feel the pressure from every side—weight from the top, and competition from the sides and bottom. This pressure is what keeps the blocks in their nice, square shape, and in their positions. The pyramid is built upon, and its order depends upon, oppression.

The devastating effects

What is the effect on the blocks? How does it feel to be under so much pressure? How do the blocks feel about being in the pyramid? Let's meet five blocks, located at different levels of the pyramid, and try to understand the pressures they feel.

The Pyramid

At the bottom of the pyramid, meet Bud Block. He's a convict. He has dark skin, a muscular body covered with scars, and a long criminal record. His father left home before he was born, his mother died when he was young, and he grew up on the streets. With no family, he felt strong peer pressure to join a gang. With no job, he felt the pressure of an empty stomach and no roof over his head. Living in a city, he felt the pressure of materialism all around him, showing him everything he didn't have. Selling drugs to make money, he felt the pressure of crime bosses and police. Here in his cellblock, he feels the pressure of the other inmates, the guards, and the four walls closing him in.

Beatrice Block is a few levels higher up the pyramid. She's a mother of five children. Her skin is brown, her clothes are worn out, and her face is tired. She works 12 hours per day in the fields while her mother looks after the younger children. Illiterate herself, she wants her children to attend high school and move up the pyramid, but there doesn't seem much hope. School is expensive, and her husband drinks and gambles away her small income. The oldest son now works in the fields too, and the oldest daughter was lured away to the city where she got trapped into prostitution. Once she felt the future was bright, but now all she sees is darkness.

In the middle of the pyramid we find Ben Block. He's tall, white, and athletic. He works as a sales manager in a pharmaceutical company. Every day at work he faces pressure from all sides—the economy is down, sales are off, and his

23

division is in bad shape. His boss has set unrealistic goals, and expects Ben to meet them. If he doesn't, there are three or four junior managers ready to jump in and take his place. If he loses this job, he's sunk, because he's already taken out a second mortgage on his house, he just had his car repaired, and his 5 major credit cards are spent to the limit. So, he puts in long hours, working nights and weekends, to meet his sales goals. But it's taking a toll on his family life. He hardly ever sees the children, and in what little time he has with his wife they end up arguing and fighting. He feels like he's losing a frantic race with no finish line in sight.

Near the very top of the pyramid are Betty and Bartholomew Block. They live at a level of comfort and privilege that kings of ancient times could only dream of. With an army of servants, mansions in several different countries, luxury cars, a private jet and yacht, they live and move in physical paradise. Yet they, too, feel pressure. They are afraid. They are afraid of losing it all. Deep down inside they know that they are no better than Bud, Beatrice or Ben. And they fear that one day those three, or others like them, will figure that out for themselves, and try to take their place. So they build walls to protect themselves, and they try to block out the pain and suffering of the other, less fortunate blocks below them in the pyramid.

Thus we find that in our pyramid of oppression, all the blocks, from top to bottom, feel pressure. The pressure at the bottom is mostly a result of domination from above. Moving up the pyramid, the pressure of domination gives way to the pressure of competition. At the top, the pressure is the need to keep the pyramid together, and the fear of what will happen if it comes apart. Whether they are dominated, competing, or dominating others, all the blocks are oppressed.

Response to pressure

Feeling this pressure, the blocks respond. They either resist, run away, or comply. In any case, they must create tough walls to protect themselves. The inescapable pressure of the pyramid molds them into tough, resistant cubes. The greater the pressure, the harder they become. And the harder they become, the better they are for holding up the pyramid. From top to bottom, the model block is one that can withstand pressure, that can "take it." The ideal block is hard and stiff—completely insulated from the block next to it—even though they are packed tightly together.

An instinctive response to pressure is resistance—to fight back. To use force against force. Action and reaction. Be a man. Stand up to them. Revolt. Rebel. Start a revolution. Throw a Molotov cocktail. Destroy them. Tear down the pyramid.

And when it is torn down, then what? Blocks are still blocks. Force is still force. Using the only available model—one that has been forced into their very being—the blocks quickly rebuild the pyramid, stronger than ever. There are a few changes perhaps, but the bottom blocks usually stay at the bottom. Maybe some middle and upper blocks shift their positions.

Resistance uses all the tools of domination, including deceit: Lie. Cheat. Steal. Lie to the boss. Cheat on your income tax. Steal from the company. Hey, after all, they're lying to us, cheating us, and stealing from us, right?

Unfortunately, the tools of domination are dirty, and whoever uses them, for whatever purpose, finds himself building the pyramid of oppression stronger and higher. Lies and deceit create distrust between the blocks, reinforcing their walls with suspicion and contempt.

A more passive form of resistance is to sulk. Do the minimum. Show no initiative. Don't participate. Don't learn. Play stupid. Act dumb. Say yes, yes, yes, to the master, and then do a little as possible, or nothing at all.

But this doesn't break down the pyramid. If anything, it also strengthens it because the top blocks become more convinced that the bottom blocks don't deserve better. They are just stupid, lazy, ignorant blocks, and belong at the bottom of the pyramid.

These forms of resistance, the instinctive and spontaneous responses to domination, serve little purpose than to reinforce the pyramid. As a block resists the pressure of domination, it conforms more and more to the ideal block-like shape and durability so necessary for the pyramid's structure. Thus the oppressive nature of the pyramid serves to preserve and maintain itself.

As an alternative to resisting, some blocks try to escape. Physically, they run away, join a commune, ride the rails, or travel around the world on a shoe-string. Mentally they escape through drugs, alcohol, television, social media, or frenzied work. The escapees are often isolated, sitting on the fringes of society. The pyramid may lose a few blocks, but its basic structure is hardly weakened.

Tragically, there are many who lack the ability to escape or resist, and yet are deeply affected by the dysfunctional nature of the pyramid. Victims of a system they had no hand in creating, they are the starving child, the homeless, the mentally ill, and the abused elder. The pyramid was not built for them, and they lose their place within it.

But most blocks survive. They don't try to resist or escape. They comply. They learn early on that "you can't change the system," and so they do their best to work within it, obeying the rules and trying to work their way up. Whether they like the pyramid or not, they comply with it, which can only reinforce it.

Our pyramid, then, seems to be a fairly durable model of social organization. It has stood the test of time, having been expanded, refined, and consolidated for thousands of years. It is orderly, providing a place for every well-behaved block. And it has many built-in features that allow it to preserve and enhance its structure. On the other hand, it is oppressive. The pressure of domination required to build and maintain it molds people into blocks. The weight from the top presses them down, competition from both sides presses them in, and the pressure from below threatens their position. Responding to this pressure, the blocks grow calloused and hard against each other. Hence, the oppression within the pyramid helps preserve its form.

So where does that leave us? How are we going to loosen the knot of oppression in this pyramid-style of social organization? The answer is not to be found within the pyramid, but it will have a powerful effect on it.

The Globe

Every thousand years or so, an event takes place that shakes the pyramid to its foundations. The very mention of this event is the worst nightmare of every top block. Middle blocks, in their typical competitive way, are divided over the event. But the bottom blocks look upon the event, as it occurs and long after its passing, with awe, hope, and wonder. The event is the advent of the Globe.

The Globe is perfectly spherical in shape. It doesn't fit well among the blocks. It doesn't stack, and you can't pile any blocks upon it. It doesn't sit still, either. It rolls around at will throughout the pyramid, causing upsets and turmoil in the carefully ordered system. It is a menace to the entire structure of the pyramid.

Whenever the Globe appears, the top blocks declare a state of emergency. They marshal all their forces to exterminate it. They call on their most loyal guards among the middle blocks, to summon the masses of bottom blocks. They mobilize the whole pyramid to put the Globe at the very bottom, hoping that with the full weight of all the blocks, they can squeeze it into conformity. But it doesn't work. The Globe maintains its perfect sphere.

The real threat to the pyramid is not the Globe itself, however. One small sphere, no matter how round, will not bring down the pyramid. The threat is what the Globe does, because the Globe is born into the pyramid with a mission. Its mission is to transform the blocks. It has been made round and whole like the sun, and it brings a ray of hope, a life-giving spirit, an ocean of relief to the blocks. It tells them that their destiny is to shine like the sun, to be round, free, and radiant. It offers guidance to any block who wants to transform itself into a globe.

To become a globe, says the Globe, we have to understand that life has many dimensions—physical and spiritual. We have been created to experience and enjoy all these dimensions. The spiritual dimensions of life are based on love from the Creator.

If there is a Creator, after all, if we are not all just random collections of atoms and molecules, if there is a purpose to our lives beyond involuntary slavery, if we truly have free will —then the will of the Creator must be the source of that will within us, and the love of that Creator must be the source of our ability to love. Spirit begets spirit, does it not? Where else could this love come from?

This love is given to us freely to enjoy, and it pervades the whole creation. Because this love is so free and so abundant, the spiritual dimensions of life are free, abundant, and full of love.

A Divine Messenger

The Globe, for us, is a divine Messenger, or Teacher, who lives among us. Through His[1] own example, the Messenger teaches us how to love, how to develop our spiritual nature, and thus how to be free. The Messenger helps us to establish a relationship, a bond of love with our Creator. In this relationship, the Creator offers to love us, and sends the Messenger to guide us. If we accept the offer, and willingly follow the guidance of the Messenger, we open our hearts and grow in our ability to love. This draws us closer to our Creator, effectively binding us to Him. Ironically, in this bond of love we find true freedom—freedom of the spirit. Through this bond we improve our lives, become better human beings, and free ourselves from oppression.

So how does it work? First we need to recognize the Messenger as a true representative from our loving Creator. Once we do this, we can willingly accept His teachings as authoritative, because we realize that His guidance is based on love for us and a deep understanding of our true needs. Authority comes from the Author, the One who wrote the book of creation. This authority is based on love, understanding, and attraction, not the force of domination.

The next step is for us to break out of the walls we have built around ourselves to resist the forces of domination, competition, and the pressure of the pyramid structure.

Now we must learn not to resist. Following the Messenger's example, we learn not to use force, not to be violent, and not to react with anger against domination. We begin to employ a higher power of love. The love of the Creator gives us the power to forgive, to overlook anger and hatred, to endure the weight of domination, no matter how painful—with love, true love—even for those who would dominate us.

We drop another tool of resistance: deceit. We rise above lying, cheating and stealing. We become truthful and trustworthy, even when we are lied to or stolen from. The spiritual freedom we begin to experience lifts us out of our sullenness, stubbornness, and inertia brought on by oppressive forces. We begin to feel light and free.

Those of us who used to escape through alcohol, drugs, or other diversions find that with love in our hearts we can overcome the pain of domination. Any of us who had hardened our hearts through conflict and competition now find that we can cooperate. Those among us who had been working along within the system find we can now view our work as service, as an act of love. Each of us who follows the Messenger's guidance finds himself or herself transformed.

This is not a new story. Indeed, we know the Messengers of the past by different names: Krishna, Moses, Buddha, Christ, and Muḥammad are some of them. The people who first recognized the Messenger as being sent by the Creator became His disciples. They joined together, and named their group after the Messenger. As they followed His guidance, they found themselves being spiritually transformed. They became more loving and tolerant. They felt freer inside. They discovered that with love in their hearts they could withstand and even overcome the oppression that pushed them down.

And we might fondly wish that the good news had quickly spread from these early followers across land and sea, until it touched the hearts of everyone. But it's not quite that simple. The pyramid is not easily moved.

Reaction and Result

Whenever this Globe—this Messenger—appears, most of the people, especially those in high positions, grow alarmed. The Messenger is a threat to society as they define it. They realize that if enough people join this group, the whole pyramid will collapse. Whatever position they have, all they have worked and struggled for, will be lost, because they know you can't stack globes on top of each other.

So, when they realize that the Messenger will not conform, cannot be squeezed into shape, and insists on guiding the people to develop themselves as spiritual beings, they get out their toolbox of domination and unleash the full fury of its force and deceit upon Him and His disciples. The Messenger Himself is exterminated and the followers are dispersed. But His influence and life-giving spirit continue to inspire them. They regroup and start to teach in His name.

One by one, and then group by group, as the people learn about the Messenger and His guidance, they accept and follow it, loosening the knot of oppression in their lives. Over several generations, the spirit of the Messenger starts to pervade the whole society, and eventually the majority of the people accept Him and honor Him. Stories are written about Him; songs are sung in His memory. The name of the Messenger is found adorning every institution and group. Society itself becomes a monument to the Messenger. And yet, somehow, the pyramid structure remains intact. In a sense nothing really changes, because another influence is at work.

From the time of the Messenger's passing, the memory and understanding of His guidance begins to get confused and lost. As different individuals and groups among the followers remember His life and message differently, they argue and dispute with each other. Those who seem to remember best, and argue most convincingly, soon become leaders, or priests. They appoint themselves as the official interpreters of the Messenger, and over time begin to mix their own ideas in with the original guidance. To consolidate understanding they introduce standard interpretations and dogmas, and to appeal to the uneducated people they encourage fanciful mythologies of the Messenger that obscure His message. Since they have no other way to organize themselves, they use the pyramid model, only now with a hierarchy of priests.

The priests find their position at the top of society comfortable, and the name of the Messenger becomes a handy tool to keep themselves there. As the centuries pass, the material comforts of status and power overwhelm the priests so completely that they entirely lose sight of the purpose of the Messenger's guidance, and focus their efforts on maintaining their positions. Instead of the blocks being transformed into globes, the pyramid eventually wins by transforming the globes back into blocks.

After another thousand years or so, however, just when things appear to be totally hopeless, when the poor and weak are groaning from the weight on top of them, when the middle class is deep in competition, and the iron fist of domination is strongest; just when society seems hopelessly dysfunctional, the Messenger appears again. He has more divine teachings and as before, looks like an ordinary person. The priests reject Him out of hand. They denounce Him, calling Him a false prophet because He doesn't correspond to their ideas and myths. Fearful of losing their positions, they encourage the ignorant masses to destroy the Messenger and His followers. But the spirit of the Messenger and His message remain. His example and guidance start to loosen the knot of oppression, and a new cycle begins.

So, is that it? Is human civilization just a continuous cycle of oppression and release, of despair and hope, of tightening and loosening the knot? Is there no end or conclusion? Is there no real progress?

A New Social Model

Actually, there is progress. The Messenger's teachings are so powerful that even at the point of deepest oppression, certain individuals remember the message. They maintain their humanity, showing love and compassion in the face of domination. And as a whole, society advances too. With each Messenger, some of the guidance remains with us as we incorporate it into our lives. The next Messenger then picks up from that point and brings us another step higher in our development. Then finally, after thousands of years, we reach a level where we are ready to break out of the pyramid model altogether—and establish a new social model.

That time has come. Humanity has reached a point in its social development where a new model is necessary. We can no longer continue under the domination of a pyramid structure. As individuals we are more spiritually mature now, and our society requires a more sophisticated model.

The most recent Messenger included a blueprint for the new model in His teachings. To make sure the ideas don't get lost, He wrote them down. So we don't get confused, He appointed an Interpreter. To prevent a hierarchy of priests, he abolished the priesthood. And in addition to guidance that will help us become fully human—spiritual and physical—beings, He gave guidance for building a new social structure that will lead to a quantum leap in human civilization.

Any structure needs some kind of cohesive power or force to hold it together. In the case of the pyramid, the force of cohesion was the power of oppression. In the new society, the force of cohesion is the power of attraction—the power of unity and love. This is the attraction between the people and the Messenger. As each of us grows to love Him and follow His teachings, a bond of unity is built between ourselves and Him. If it were a physical structure, we could think of the Messenger acting as a hub, with bonds of love radiating out in all directions, each bond linking one of us to Himself.

What also happens is that we build bonds of unity between each other. We join together, and of our own free will, we form resilient bonds and links of love, friendship, fellowship, and unity. With the Messenger's guidance, each of us becomes a hub of sorts, radiating firm, flexible bonds between each other—long and short. A new structure is born, taking the form of a geodesic, an overarching dome constructed of many interconnected globes. Each person, or globe, is connected at the center to the Messenger, the Globe. The structure grows organically, adding ever more globes which are always connected to each other and to the Messenger through bonds of love.

This new social order is superior to the pyramid in several ways. First, it is built on the principle of voluntary participation. Individuals willingly, lovingly, join together, creating bonds of unity that give the structure its strength. The power of unity holding it together is much stronger than the weight of gravity and force of domination that holds up the pyramid.

Second, everyone participates fully, in his or her own way. Each globe is slightly different, sits in a unique position, and has something special to offer the group. This diversity is unified, however, as each globe is fully connected, simultaneously united in many interlocking bonds.

Third, in a geodesic dome, the stress is shared and supported by all the members, rather than the weakest members. That said, the most essential globes are those at the bottom, whose combined bonds form a foundation circle that holds the whole dome together. Without this bond, other bonds higher up could break and the dome would collapse. The strongest, most able, most dedicated globes, although located at the bottom of the dome, attain true merit by performing this vital service.

Like the pyramid, our new geodesic style of structure is organized, natural and efficient, but it embodies a higher level of natural law than a pyramid. We can think of it as the difference between an inert mineral and a living organism. For example, in nature we find pyramid-shaped crystals, whose atoms are aligned together in a regular pattern, producing a beautiful shape, demonstrating a static form of intelligence. Our geodesic patterns, on the other hand, suggest a higher, more interactive form of organization. In principle they are more like the human brain, whose neurons are joined together in very complex patterns that can sustain dynamic intelligence.

The efficiency of the pyramid is created through uniformity and a top-down command structure. All the blocks follow the leader. A similar natural phenomenon is the organization and power of a magnet. As all the molecules are aligned in a uniform way, their combined charge is very strong. This is efficiency at the mineral level of creation. However, in a society of fully developed human beings, each is intelligent and has much more to offer than the dipolarity of a single molecule. Our new social structure gains its efficiency by tapping that potential. Although seemingly awkward and difficult to manage, the rich diversity of human nature that is released when the knot of oppression is untied can create an undreamed-of level of achievement and beauty. When each of us is free inside, we develop our talents, and without threat of force or fear of violence, we work willingly and lovingly to achieve the purpose of our society.

All we have to do is recognize the Messenger and follow His guidance. The rest of this book explains in greater detail how we can loosen the knot of oppression and build a new social order, based on the guidance of the two most recent Messengers sent by the Creator: The Báb and Bahá'u'lláh.

Notes

1. The Messengers we know of in recent history, such as Moses, Jesus, Muḥammad, Krishna and Buddha were male, but there may have been female Messengers in the past, and could there be in the future. I use the male pronoun for convenience only.

The Báb

"O peoples of the earth! Verily the resplendent Light of God hath appeared in your midst, invested with this unerring Book, that ye may be guided aright to the ways of peace and, by the leave of God, step out of the darkness into the light and onto this far-extended Path of Truth."[1] - The Báb

High on the top of Máh-Kú Mountain, near the city of Khuy in Northeastern Persia sits a castle in ruins. A stone fortress with four towers, it looks over the Araxes river at a point where Persia, Turkey, and Armenia come together. That area is known as the land of the Kurds, a people unified by a common religion, culture, and language, but divided by borders of other nations.

A hundred and fifty years ago the castle functioned as the last outpost of the Kingdom of Persia. From this vantage point a small garrison of a few men could see and report armies advancing from Russia or Turkey. But it was not considered pleasant duty for a Persian soldier. It was far from family and friends, far from the comfort of the great Persian cities. The castle was made of stone, with little protection from the cold mountain winds. The local villagers offered small comfort, since the Kurds in the area had a reputation for being as wild and inhospitable as their land. And as believers in Sunní Islám, they were bitter enemies of the Shí'ih Persians.

In the spring of 1847 a man named 'Alí Khán was the keeper of the castle of Máh-Kú. He was a strong, proud man, who carried out his orders with an iron fist. He was the ideal man for the job, because although he was a Persian, his mother was a Kurd. He understood the ways of the Kurds, and was accepted and respected by the villagers, even though he represented a government they hated.

One day that spring 'Alí Khán received orders to guard a Prisoner, whose title was the Báb. This "Báb" was considered very dangerous, a revolutionary, a threat to the stability of the country. 'Alí Khán's orders were to keep Him in strict confinement, and he was going to follow those orders to the letter. When the Prisoner arrived, there was a great commotion in the village. The people gathered around, curious to get a good look at Him. They had heard all sorts of rumors. But they were surprised. This was no fanatical madman talking of revolution. This was no sword-carrying radical. He was a mild-mannered young man who spoke so politely, so sincerely to them, that he completely won them over.

"The turbulent spirits of this unruly people were soon subdued by the gentle manners of the Báb, and their hearts were softened by the ennobling influence of His love. Their pride was humbled by His unexampled modesty, and their unreasoning arrogance mellowed by the wisdom of His words."[2]

'Alí Khán, however, reprimanded the people for associating with his Prisoner. He forbade them to talk to Him. He escorted the Báb and His two companions through the castle grounds gates. Bolting them securely, he took the prisoners up the steep road to the castle and locked them securely in their respective cells.

'Alí Khán's orders were that no-one was to visit the Báb, and He was not permitted out of His cell. One of His two companions was allowed to go into the town to buy food or supplies, always accompanied by a guard. There he could sometimes meet with followers of the Báb who had made the arduous journey to this forsaken outpost to meet Him. But 'Alí Khán wouldn't even allow those followers to spend the night in the town of Máh-Kú. And so it went for the first few weeks.

But one day a strange thing happened. Early one morning the guards heard the voice of 'Alí Khán at the gate, shouting at them to open it. When they did so, he rushed angrily past them up to the castle and ran straight to the Báb's prison cell. But as he entered the room, his entire attitude changed to amazement, humility, and wonder. Anxious and fearful, he approached the Báb and said these words:

"Deliver me from my perplexity. I adjure You, by the Prophet of God, Your illustrious Ancestor, to dissipate my doubts, for their weight has well-nigh crushed my heart. I was riding through the wilderness and was approaching the gate of the town, when, it being the hour of dawn, my eyes suddenly beheld You standing by the side of the river engaged in offering Your prayer. With outstretched arms and upraised eyes, You were invoking the name of God. I stood still and watched You. I was waiting for You to terminate Your devotions that I might approach and rebuke You for having ventured to leave the castle without my leave. In Your communion with God, You seemed so wrapt in worship that You were utterly forgetful of Yourself. I quietly approached You; in Your state of rapture, You remained wholly unaware of my presence. I was suddenly seized with great fear and recoiled at the thought of awakening You from Your ecstasy. I decided to leave You, to proceed to the guards and to reprove them for their negligent conduct. I soon found out, to my amazement, that both the outer and inner gates were closed. They were opened at my request, I was ushered into Your presence, and now find You, to my wonder, seated before me. I am utterly confounded. I know not whether my reason has deserted me."[3]

The Báb replied, saying, "What you have witnessed is true and undeniable. You belittled this Revelation and have contemptuously disdained its Author. God, the All-Merciful, desiring not to afflict you with His punishment, has willed to reveal to your eyes the Truth. By His Divine interposition, He has instilled into your heart the love of His chosen One, and caused you to recognize the unconquerable power of His Faith."[4]

From that moment onwards, 'Alí Khán was a changed man. He swore his undying allegiance to the Báb and His Cause. There was nothing he couldn't do to make the Báb's stay in the castle-prison more comfortable, despite receiving strict orders to the contrary. He often came by to visit the Báb, bringing gifts of rare and expensive fruit. He relaxed his vigil to the point where the gates of the castle were open all day to receive the Báb's followers, and they were allowed to stay as long as they wished. During this time, the Báb was busy writing, revealing scripture. As He wrote, he would chant holy verses in clear, melodic tones that echoed down from the mountain to the village. Hearing His voice, meditating on His words, the villagers felt their love for the Báb grow day by day.

Transforming the Hearts

Who was this Man, this Personage, that had such power to transform hearts, even of His own jailer? His given name was Siyyid 'Alí-Muḥammad. He was born in 1819 in Shíráz, Persia. His father died when he was a baby, and he was raised by his mother's brother. As a child, He showed such remarkable wisdom and intelligence that school teachers were unable to teach Him. Upon reaching adulthood, He became a merchant with a reputation for excellence, but devoted most of His time to prayer, meditation and worshiping God.

In 1844 Siyyid 'Alí-Muḥammad announced to another young man (who then became His first disciple) that He was a

Messenger of God, the Promised One of Islám. He took the title "The Báb," which means "the Gate." He was the spiritual gate to open the way for another, greater Divine Messenger, soon to follow. He had come to prepare the hearts of the people so they would accept that next Messenger. His mission was to transform the hearts.

And transform He did. People from all walks of life —students, workers, businessmen and bureaucrats, poets, housewives and servants, rich and poor—were attracted to Him. First, a group of 17 men and one woman who had been seeking the Promised One for years recognized the Báb without being told. They became His disciples, named the 18 Letters of the Living. Their mission was to travel throughout the land and proclaim the advent of the New Day, the coming of the Promised One.

"O My beloved friends!" the Báb told them at their departure, "You are the bearers of the name of God in this Day. You have been chosen as the repositories of His mystery. It behooves each one of you to manifest the attributes of God, and to exemplify by your deeds and words the signs of His righteousness, His power and glory. The very members of your body must bear witness to the loftiness of your purpose, the integrity of your life, the reality of your faith, and the exalted character of your devotion...."[5]

They had their job cut out for them. Persia in those days was probably one of the most oppressive countries in the world. The Sháh (king) held absolute power. His hands controlled the life and death, trial, punishment, and economic fate of every person in the land. The judicial system was arbitrary, and the penal system brutal. Criminals were commonly tortured, beaten, and executed in such horrifying ways as crucifixion, burning, having their bodies torn apart, and being fired from cannons. The Sháh's administration was corrupt, functioning on a system of bribes and favors. The smoke of flattery and deceit generated by his bureaucrats and ministers was so dense that he often lost sight of the affairs of state altogether. Furthermore, Persia at that time functioned as a church state. The religious clergy, or mullás, held a great deal of political power, both locally and nationally, as representatives of God, Muḥammad, and Islám. They trained their oratorical powers on the simple, unquestioning faith of the common people, locking them in a dogmatic stranglehold. This was a matter of self-interest, since much of the mullás' power, income, and comfortable lifestyle depended upon the support of the masses.

Against these odds, the Letters of the Living set out. The radiance and purity of their burning hearts poured like a brilliant shower of sparks into the cold, dark, wasteland of a dead society. The light in their eyes and their warmth of devotion to the Báb kindled a glow of hope in their listeners. Through each village and town they passed, they left behind shining embers that quickly fanned into flames of love. In a few months the number of Bábís (believers in the Báb) began growing by the hundreds. Word spread quickly that there was a new Prophet, a new Messenger, and new religion in the land. The Promised One had come!

The Báb's teachings turned the world of Islám on its head. Although affirming the divine station of Muḥammad, The Báb claimed that His Own latter Revelation was now needed to bring mankind to a new level of civilization. He changed the Islamic laws of marriage, divorce, fasting, and inheritance, and established a new calendar. He chastised the Islamic clergy for their failure to abide by the true precepts of their Faith, and gave profound interpretations to various religious themes such as heaven, hell, judgement day, and resurrection. Above all, He repeatedly emphasized the immanent advent of "Him Whom God shall make manifest."

The mullás felt threatened by these teachings. A few of them investigated the claims of the Báb, and believed in him. But the overwhelming majority denounced Him as a heretic, a false prophet, and a trouble-maker. As soon as the Letters of the Living began to spread word of this new Message, the mullás opposed it. They instigated opposition among their congregations by spreading slanderous lies and preaching malicious sermons in the mosques. They gave free license to mobs to attack and kill the Báb's followers and plunder their possessions. And they approached government officials, deceiving them that this movement was political in nature, designed to cause instability in the land and ultimately to overthrow the Sháh.

As a result, the Bábís suffered the oppressive weight of both the religious and political regimes. They were imprisoned, beaten, tortured, and put to death in indescribably hideous ways. They were cut off from their families, stripped of all possessions, and cast out of their homes and towns. The Báb Himself was put in prison. A group of 313 of His followers, including several Letters of the Living, made an attempt to travel across the north of Persia to visit Him, but they were stopped on their route by mullá-incited mobs. In self-defense, they retired to a religious shrine in an area called Ṭabarsí, and built a fortification to protect themselves.

For many months they were besieged, first by angry citizens, then local militias and the prince's soldiers, and finally by federal troops. Although the Bábís were mainly religious scholars, tradespeople, and villagers, with no military training, they made several pre-emptive sorties on their attackers, scattering and routing whole battalions of professional soldiers armed with guns and cannon and numbering in the thousands. The Bábís rode on horseback and carried swords, but what struck fear in the hearts of their adversaries was their victory cry: Yá Ṣáḥibu'z-Zamán!—He is the Lord of the Age!

Finally, they were cheated into surrendering. Lured out of their fort by false promises on the Holy Qur'án that they could continue their journey unharmed, they were disarmed and executed, one by one. Only a few escaped to tell the story. This was just part of a larger campaign to exterminate the

Faith of the Báb in Persia. All told, over 20,000 Bábís were martyred, including all of the Letters of the Living. Finally the Báb Himself was executed in 1850. The mullás had done their job well. This strange, disturbing uprising was quelled, and life would continue as it had.

Or so they thought. The Báb, too, had done His job well. The flame he had lit was not totally burned out. The hearts were prepared. The Gate had opened. The next Messenger was yet to come.

Notes

1. The Báb, *Selections from the Writings of The Báb*, p 61
2. Nabíl-i-A'zam, *The Dawn Breakers*, p 244-5
3. Ibid, p 247
4. Ibid.
5. Ibid, p 92

Bahá'u'lláh

"The Ancient Beauty hath consented to be bound with chains that mankind may be released from its bondage, and hath accepted to be made a prisoner within this most mighty Stronghold that the whole world may attain unto true liberty."[1] - Bahá'u'lláh

Let's take a walk. The year is 1853, and we're in the palace of the S͟háh of Persia. He sends his guard to escort us. The guard takes us through shady courtyards, past bubbling fountains, and down long pillared hallways, ornately decorated with inlaid mother-of-pearl mosaics. Then he leads us down a stone passageway that ends at a heavy steel door. The guard lights a torch, and with a jangle of keys, opens the door, and we walk down a long flight of steps. The air becomes musty and dank. Crossing a short landing, we continue down another flight. We begin to notice a strange smell coming up from down below. We reach another landing, and descend yet more steps. At the bottom we come to another massive door, barred and bolted shut. The guard hands us his torch as he opens the rusty locks one by one. Slowly he swings the door open.

A horrible stench greets us—the smell of urine, fecal matter, rotting clothes and unwashed bodies. In the dim torchlight we see dozens of men, chained and packed together in the cold darkness. They are thieves, murderers, and bandits—some of the most vicious criminals of the kingdom. And there, over to one side, seated in two rows, are some 40 Bábís. Our guard calls one of them by name. He leaps to his feet, overcome with joy. When the guard unchains him, he embraces his fellow prisoners, one by one. From one Prisoner, who is doubled over by the weight of a 50-kilo chain around His neck, he receives a special blessing, and a pair of shoes. The man, delirious with joy, follows the guard up the steps—to his execution. The Prisoner, now barefoot, watches him, prays for him, and knows that he will soon be in paradise. This Prisoner is Bahá'u'lláh.

Bahá'u'lláh was no stranger to the palace of the Sháh. His late father was a member of the Sháh's court, one of his most trusted ministers. Bahá'u'lláh (whose given name was Mírzá Ḥusayn-'Alí) was born in the Núr region of Persia in 1817, and spent His childhood in Tehran, the capital city, as well as on His father's estates in Núr, located in the northern province of Mázindarán, near the Caspian Sea. Like the Báb, young Ḥusayn-'Alí was sent home from school because his teachers quickly discovered that he possessed an innate knowledge and wisdom far greater than their own. As a young man, he refused to assume a political career like his father, but chose instead to share the family wealth with the poor and needy. No one was turned away from his door or table. He offered solace and financial support to all who asked. Businessmen came to him for professional advice, religious scholars for insight, and lawyers for guidance in resolving disputes. Everyone who approached him came away satisfied, and all agreed that Mírzá Ḥusayn-'Alí was the Father of the Poor.

In the summer of 1844 Mírzá Ḥusayn-'Alí received a visitor sent by the First Letter of the Living of the Báb. This messenger gave him a scroll, a copy of some of the Báb's first writings. Upon reading those writings, Mírzá Ḥusayn-'Alí instantly recognized their divine origin, and from that time onward became a strong supporter of the Cause of the Báb.

He took the title Bahá'u'lláh (which means "The Glory of God") in 1848 during a conference with Letters of the Living and other Bábís in a small village called Badasht. There each of the Bábís was given a title, unaware that it had come from Bahá'u'lláh. There they were guided to a deeper understanding of their new Faith. Although He never met the Báb face to face, Bahá'u'lláh played a key role in the conference and in the years to come as a role model and wise counsel, a solid pillar of faith during the turbulent and oppressive times that faced the Bábís.

After most of the leading Bábís were martyred at Ṭabarsí, and the Báb Himself was executed in 1850, the mullás were determined to stamp out every trace of the Bábí Faith. Aided by the Sháh and his government, they imprisoned, tortured and killed as many Bábís as they could. Bahá'u'lláh, acknowledged as a spiritual leader and fearless spokesperson for the Bábís, did not pass unnoticed, but He had many supporters in the S̲h̲áh's court. Finally, accused under false pretenses, He was thrown into this abandoned water tank three stories below the S̲h̲áh"s palace, named the "Síyáh-Chál," or "Black Pit," the worst dungeon of the land. Here, hoped Bahá'u'lláh's enemies, He would perish.

The Revelation

But instead, it was here in the most odious prison of Persia that Bahá'u'lláh received His divine summons, His Revelation. Afterward, He wrote the following passages that give us some hint of the experience:

> During the days I lay in the prison of Ṭihrán, though the galling weight of the chains and the stench-filled air allowed Me but little sleep, still in those infrequent moments of slumber, I felt as if something flowed from the crown of My head over My breast, even as a mighty torrent that precipitateth itself upon the earth from the summit of a lofty mountain. Every limb of My body would, as a result, be set afire. At such moments My tongue recited what no man could bear to hear.[2]

> While engulfed in tribulations I heard a most wondrous, a most sweet voice, calling above My head. Turning My face, I beheld a Maiden—the embodiment of the remembrance of the name of My Lord—suspended in the air before Me. ... Pointing with her finger unto

My head, she addressed all who are in heaven and all who are on earth, saying: "By God! This is the Best-Beloved of the worlds, and yet ye comprehend not. This is the Beauty of God amongst you, and the power of His sovereignty within you, could ye but understand. This is the Mystery of God and His Treasure, the Cause of God and His Glory unto all who are in the kingdom of Revelation and of creation, if ye be of them that perceive.[3]

Although each of His companions in the Síyáh-Chál were martyred one by one, Bahá'u'lláh's life was spared. After four months the Sháh had to accept the fact that this Prisoner was innocent of any crime, and so, giving in to pressure of friends and family, he released Him. When Bahá'u'lláh emerged from the prison His neck was scarred and His body was doubled over from the weight of the chains. His hair had turned white and His face had aged. But He had little time to rest or recover His health. He, His family, and some close friends were given one month to depart to 'Iráq, banished from their native land of Persia.

The exiles traveled in winter by foot and on horseback through the snow-covered mountains, reaching Baghdád in early spring. Over the next ten years Bahá'u'lláh gradually became the recognized leader of the Bábí community, both among the friends in Baghdád, as well as many of the Bábís in Persia. As time passed, more and more of them would come to visit their fellow Bábís in Baghdád, and all were greatly devoted to Bahá'u'lláh. All during this time Bahá'u'lláh kept secret that He was the One the Báb had spoken about, He Whom God will make manifest.

Nevertheless, Bahá'u'lláh began to reveal the Word of God, chanting and writing prayers, meditations, tablets (essays), and books. He used to visit a tea-house daily and converse with the townspeople, as well as walk along the banks of the Tigris River. All who listened to Him or read His Writings were amazed at His eloquence, moderation, and penetrating insight. He answered every question, no matter how difficult or perplexing, with a wisdom that astonished the listeners. One time He received a letter from an uncle of the Báb. The uncle wanted to know how it was possible that his own nephew, who was apparently just an ordinary man, could be a Messenger of God, the Promised One of Islám.

The Book of Certitude

The answer that Bahá'u'lláh gave came in the form of a book. Revealed in less than 2 days and 2 nights, this book is called *The Book of Certitude* (*Kitáb-i-Íqán*), and it explains why every Messenger of God is rejected and oppressed by the people He has come to guide. It tells how all the Messengers in religious history appeared as ordinary men, which caused confusion among the people. "How could this man that we've known all our lives be a Prophet of God?" they would ask. Bahá'u'lláh gives examples of Noah, Abraham, Moses, Christ, Muḥammad and other prophets, and how each of them faced rejection and strong opposition. And He explains how the individuals most responsible for this rejection, either through ignorance or desire for power, were the religious leaders.

> Leaders of religion, in every age, have hindered their people from attaining the shores of eternal salvation, inasmuch as they held the reins of authority in their mighty grasp. Some for lust of leadership, others through want of knowledge and understanding, have been the cause of the deprivation of the people. By their sanction and authority, every Prophet of God hath drunk from the chalice of sacrifice and winged His flight unto the heights of glory.[4] - Bahá'u'lláh

In *The Book of Certitude*, Bahá'u'lláh goes on to explain that scripture is written in symbolic language. This symbolism is a test, a way to see if we really understand spiritual ideas, or if we are thinking and acting along material lines only. The majority of religious leaders, according to Bahá'u'lláh, failed the test. For example, the Pharisees of Jesus's time were expecting the Messiah to conquer the East and the West, sit on the throne of David, and establish a peace wherein wolves and lambs would drink from the same fountain. They didn't see or couldn't accept that Jesus was conquering the hearts of men through the Holy Spirit, establishing an everlasting spiritual Kingdom, and that all races and tribes would gather to drink from the fountain of His Gospel. So they crucified Him. They failed the test because they didn't listen to Jesus's explanation of the true meaning of scripture. If they had listened, things would have gone differently.

> Had they sought with a humble mind from the Manifestations of God in every Dispensation the true meaning of these words revealed in the sacred books . . . they surely would have been guided to the light of the Sun of Truth, and would have discovered the mysteries of divine knowledge and wisdom.[5] - Bahá'u'lláh

This lack of understanding of the true nature of God's Messengers has been a source of great suffering for humanity. Look how Jews, Christians, and Muslims have become bitter enemies, almost since the birth of their respective religions. How many people needlessly suffered and died during the Crusades, the Inquisition, and the Holocaust? Disputes over religion remain one of the biggest causes of animosity and conflict today—in Northern Ireland, former Yugoslavia, the Middle East, India, and many other parts of the world. All this conflict has given religion a bad name. Some people have become so frustrated that they have turned away from religion altogether.

But there is an alternative. In *The Book of Certitude*, Bahá'u'lláh goes on to explain how all of God's Messengers, or Manifestations, are fundamentally the same. Each one had a different name, spoke a different language, and gave social teachings necessary for different societies at different levels of development. But each of them came from the same God, spoke with the same authority, and had the same essential message: that God created us, loves us, and has provided for our happiness, growth, and spiritual fulfillment. We just need to listen and follow the Messenger.

> Inasmuch as these Birds of the Celestial Throne are all sent down from the heaven of the Will of God, and as they all arise to proclaim His irresistible Faith, they therefore are regarded as one soul and the same person. For they all drink from the one Cup of the love of God, and all partake of the fruit of the same Tree of Oneness. These Manifestations of God have each a twofold station. One is the station of pure abstraction and essential unity.[6] - Bahá'u'lláh

> The other is the station of distinction, and pertaineth to the world of creation and to the limitations thereof. In this respect, each Manifestation of God hath a distinct individuality, a definitely prescribed mission, a predestined Revelation, and specially designed limitations. Each one of them is known by a different name, is characterized by a special attribute, fulfills a definite Mission, and is entrusted with a particular Revelation.[7]
> - Bahá'u'lláh

As time went on, the people of Baghdád grew to love and trust Bahá'u'lláh. The leaders of that city recognized

His kindness and wisdom. His popularity among the citizens and the Bábís grew, which only increased the jealously of His enemies. They saw that instead of dying out, the Bábí movement was starting to flourish once more. So through political maneuvering and manipulation of ministers, the ambassador and the Sháh of Persia himself, they convinced the Sulṭán of Turkey that Bahá'u'lláh should be exiled further, to the heart of the Turkish Empire.

The Proclamation

Upon His departure, the entire city of Baghdád turned out to bid farewell to Bahá'u'lláh. Crowds of people lined the streets and rooftops to get a final glimpse of their distinguished Visitor. Bahá'u'lláh, His family, and some of the Bábís left the city, but sojourned for more than a week in the grounds of a large garden nearby. The garden was called "Riḍván," meaning "Paradise." In this garden on April 21st, 1863, Bahá'u'lláh announced to a few close followers that He was the second Messenger, as foretold by the Báb, inaugurating a new Day, bringing to mankind a new Revelation from God.

> The Revelation which, from time immemorial, hath been acclaimed as the Purpose and Promise of all the Prophets of God, and the most cherished Desire of His Messengers, hath now, by virtue of the pervasive Will of the Almighty and at His irresistible bidding, been revealed unto men.[8] - Bahá'u'lláh

Verily I say, this is the Day in which mankind can behold the Face, and hear the Voice, of the Promised One. The Call of God hath been raised, and the light of His countenance hath been lifted up upon men.[9] - Bahá'u'lláh

This is the Day whereon naught can be seen except the splendors of the Light that shineth from the face of Thy Lord, the Gracious, the Most Bountiful. Verily, We have caused every soul to expire by virtue of Our irresistible and all-subduing sovereignty. We have, then, called into being a new creation, as a token of Our grace unto men. I am, verily, the All-Bountiful, the Ancient of Days.[10] - Bahá'u'lláh

Bahá'u'lláh departed from Baghdád in triumph, so much so that even His enemies now regretted having forced His move. With His family and a few followers, He traveled overland and by the Black Sea to Constantinople (Istanbul), the capital city of the Ottoman Empire. The group lived there a few months until again the Persian clergy grew alarmed at His influence over the hearts of the people, and instigated His further exile to the city of Adrianople (Edirne). For the next five years Bahá'u'lláh lived under house arrest in that city, and there He proclaimed more openly His Message. Gradually the majority of the Bábís came to understand and recognize Him as He Whom God will make manifest, as foretold by the Báb. Instead of "Bábís," they now came to be known as "Bahá'ís" (followers of Bahá). And now, for the first time, Bahá'u'lláh proclaimed His Mission to the people in general, and especially to the kings and rulers of the world.

He addressed the kings collectively, announcing to them that He was the Messenger of God, and that they should read and heed God's Message. They were called upon to reduce their expenditures, stop oppressing their people, and administer their realms with wisdom and justice. If they ignored this Message, God would take their kingdoms away from them. Bahá'u'lláh wrote:

> O kings of the earth! Give ear unto the Voice of God, calling from this sublime, the fruit-laden Tree, that hath sprung out of the Crimson Hill, upon the holy Plain, intoning the words: 'There is none other God but He, the Mighty, the All-Powerful, the All-Wise.' ... Fear God, O concourse of kings, and suffer not yourselves to be deprived of this most sublime grace.[11]

> Beware not to deal unjustly with any one that appealeth to you, and entereth beneath your shadow. Walk ye in the fear of God, and be ye of them that lead a goodly life. Rest not on your power, your armies, and treasures.[12]

> Know ye that the poor are the trust of God in your midst. Watch that ye betray not His trust, that ye deal not unjustly with them and that ye walk not in the ways of the treacherous.[13]

God hath committed into your hands the reins of the government of the people, that ye may rule with justice over them, safeguard the rights of the down-trodden, and punish the wrong doers.[14]

If ye pay no heed unto the counsels which, in peerless and unequivocal language, We have revealed in this Tablet, Divine chastisement shall assail you from every direction, and the sentence of His justice shall be pronounced against you.[15]

Specifically, Bahá'u'lláh wrote to Napoleon III of France, Alexander II of Russia, Queen Victoria of England, William I of Prussia and Germany, Francis Joseph of the Austro-Hungarian Empire, 'Abdu'l-'Azíz of the Ottoman Empire, and Náṣiri'd-Dín Sháh of Persia, as well as Pope Pius IX. With the exception of Queen Victoria, these messages fell on deaf ears. And one by one, except for the United Kingdom of Great Britain and Ireland, these kingdoms and empires fell.

As Bahá'u'lláh boldly proclaimed His Mission, His enemies arose against Him once more. Now, not just clergy, but even a few members of His own family grew jealous of His popularity and influence. His half-brother went so far as to try to murder Him with poison. The attempt failed, but the poison was so strong that it left Bahá'u'lláh with trembling hands for the rest of His life. The Sulṭán and his ministers grew so alarmed by this and other disturbances caused by various trouble-makers that they finally decided to send Bahá'u'lláh, his family, and a few loyal followers to the worst spot in the Turkish Empire, the prison city of 'Akká.

The Most Great Prison

The City of 'Akká has a five-thousand year history, and at this time it had reached an all-time low. "'Akká, the ancient Ptolemais, the St. Jean d'Acre of the Crusaders, that had successfully defied the siege of Napoleon, had sunk, under the Turks, to the level of a penal colony to which murderers, highway robbers and political agitators were consigned from all parts of the Turkish empire. It was girt about by a double system of ramparts; was inhabited by a people whom Bahá'u'lláh stigmatized as *'the generation of vipers'*; was devoid of any source of water within its gates; was flea-infested, damp, and honey-combed with gloomy, filthy, and tortuous lanes. ... So putrid was its air that, according to a proverb, a bird when flying over it would drop dead."[16] This gruesome place Bahá'u'lláh referred to as the Most Great Prison.

The exiles arrived by boat late in the summer of 1868. The sea journey had been difficult, but 'Akká proved to be by far the worst experience the small group was to encounter. Not only was the city foul beyond description, the authorities were brutal and the inhabitants hostile. Warned by a Sultán's decree that these were dangerous criminals and enemies of Islám, the people mocked and cursed the 'God of the Persians' and His small group as they were marched through the city to the fortress/prison. There they were locked in adjoining cells, with Bahá'u'lláh isolated from the rest of the group. Their jailers gave them bad food and sold them other supplies at exorbitant prices. Most of the group immediately came down with malaria and dysentery from the filthy conditions, and three of them died. Their enemies in Persia and Turkey expected that the rest would soon meet a similar fate.

Meantime, they made sure that Bahá'u'lláh would be completely cut off from His followers. Although a few of them, with great difficulty, crossed the deserts of Arabia to visit Him, they were refused entrance. All they could do was stand outside the city looking at the windows of the prison, hoping to catch a glimpse of Bahá'u'lláh's hand waving to them.

Perhaps the most tragic event of this time was when Bahá'u'lláh lost His youngest son, Mírzá Mihdí. The young man was so devoted to his father, exemplifying such humility and purity, that Bahá'u'lláh gave him the title "The Purest Branch". He used to go up to the roof of the prison to pray and chant the Holy writings. One night he got so lost in his devotions that he accidentally fell through a hole in the roof and impaled himself on a wooden crate in the room below. As he lay bleeding to death in his father's arms, Bahá'u'lláh asked him what he wished. Mírzá Mihdí said, "I wish the people of Bahá to be able to attain your presence." Bahá'u'lláh assured him that God had granted his request, and later wrote: "I have, O my Lord, offered up that which Thou hast given Me, that Thy servants may be quickened, and all that dwell on earth be united."[17]

This incident marked the start of changes in the conditions of the prisoners. All through their hardships and deprivations, they had always shown love and respect to each other, to their guards, to the government authorities, and to the townspeople. Little by little, month by month they won their grudging respect, then admiration, and finally complete devotion. Over time the harsh decrees of the Sulṭán were interpreted more and more loosely. Not long after Mírzá Mihdí's death, the authorities granted permission for Bahá'ís from Persia to visit Bahá'u'lláh. Then, after more than two years in the prison, space was needed for a military barracks, so the exiles were removed to two rooms of a house in the city. Several years later, as the family was increasing in size, they were given more space. A few years after that they were moved to another, larger house.

The Most Holy Book

During this time, Bahá'u'lláh revealed the most important book of His Revelation, called *The Most Holy Book* (*Kitáb-i-Aqdas*). This book covered various topics, all related in one way or another to divine authority. He explained the source and meaning of divine law, how it is given for our benefit, and how it will order our society. He reiterated His call to the kings and religious authorities, telling them to accept God's Message for them. But most of the book is for us as individuals. It tells us in specific terms how to live our lives for maximum benefit, how to live in accord with the will of our Creator. The book sets out various guidelines for personal conduct, social conduct, and spiritual conduct, which, Bahá'u'lláh assures us, are the means to real freedom. He wrote:

> Say: True liberty consisteth in man's submission unto My commandments, little as ye know it. Were men to observe that which We have sent down unto them from the Heaven of Revelation, they would, of a certainty, attain unto perfect liberty.[18]
>
> O ye peoples of the world! Know assuredly that my commandments are the lamps of My loving providence among My servants, and the keys of My mercy for My creatures. Thus hath it been sent down from the heaven of the Will of your Lord, the Lord of Revelation.[19]
>
> Think not that We have revealed unto you a mere code of laws. Nay, rather, We have unsealed the choice Wine with the fingers of might and power.[20]

Final Triumph

By 1877, after nine years in the prison-city, Bahá'u'lláh and His followers had so won over the hearts of the people and the local authorities that they were prisoners in name only. The governor, court officials, and the leading religious scholars became particularly devoted to 'Abdu'l-Bahá, Bahá'u'lláh's eldest son. They often went to Him for advice. During this time 'Abdu'l-Bahá arranged to rent a large abandoned country mansion a few kilometers from the city, and set it up for Bahá'u'lláh to live in. When the time came, He and Bahá'u'lláh rode there in a carriage. Despite all the Sulṭán's decrees, despite their strict orders, neither the guards nor anyone else raised a single objection or lifted a finger as the Prisoner and His son rode out through the gates of 'Akká.

For the next two years Bahá'u'lláh lived in the mansion, and then moved to another, bigger one closer to the city, where He lived until His passing in 1892. During these 15 years Bahá'u'lláh moved freely between the mansions and 'Akká, and even traveled to Haifa and Mount Carmel, some 30 kilometers away.

Referring to this time of Bahá'u'lláh's life, 'Abdu'l-Bahá wrote:

> "Although the policy of Sulṭán 'Abdu'l-Ḥamíd was harsher than ever; although he constantly insisted on his Captive's strict confinement—still the Blessed Beauty (Bahá'u'lláh) now lived, as everyone knows, with all power and glory. Some of the time Bahá'u'lláh would spend at the Mansion, and again, at the farm village of Mazra'ih; for a while He would sojourn in Haifa, and occasionally His tent would be pitched on the heights of Mount Carmel. Friends from everywhere presented

themselves and gained an audience. The people and the government authorities witnessed it all, yet no one so much as breathed a word. And this is one of Bahá'u'lláh's greatest miracles: that He, a captive, surrounded Himself with a panoply and He wielded power. The prison changed into a palace, the jail itself became a Garden of Eden. Such a thing has not occurred in history before; no former age has seen its like: that a man confined to a prison should move about with authority and might; that one in chains should carry the fame of the Cause of God to the high heavens, should win splendid victories in both East and West, and should, by His almighty pen, subdue the world. Such is the distinguishing feature of this supreme Theophany."[21]

The tables were turned. To the kings—those who had held Him captive and others—Bahá'u'lláh had written and delivered instructions telling them how to manage their affairs, and warning them of the consequences of failing to recognize His authority. Those who rejected His message soon saw their dynasties and empires in ruins. For the leaders of religion He had revealed new spiritual guidance that necessarily required their complete allegiance or total rejection. The court advisors and clergy who denounced Him and attempted to stamp out His Faith eventually found themselves disgraced or ignored by their followers. Those who lived long enough witnessed the Bahá'í Faith propagated throughout the world. None of Bahá'u'lláh's enemies was ever willing to stand before him face to face. Many people heard lies and slander about Him, and yet no one who had direct contact with Him could deny His majesty and power.

Bahá'u'lláh ended His life on earth free from prison, but the process of loosening the knot of oppression had just begun. His teachings, guidance, and laws laid a foundation for a new way of life and new order for society. And to ensure that this guidance was properly preserved and implemented, Bahá'u'lláh established a Covenant—a direct link between Himself and the people of the world, so that each and every one of us can overcome oppression as well.

Notes

1. Bahá'u'lláh, *Gleanings from the Writings of Bahá'u'lláh*, XLV

2. Ibid, *Epistle to the Son of the Wolf*, p 22

3. Ibid, *Súriy-i-Haykal*, paragraphs 6 and 7

4. Ibid, *The Kitáb-i-Íqán*, p 15

5. Ibid, p 28

6. Ibid, p 152

7. Ibid, p 176

8. Bahá'u'lláh, *Gleanings from the Writings of Bahá'u'lláh*, III

9. Ibid, VII

10. Ibid, XIV

11. Bahá'u'lláh, *Súriy-i-Mulúk*, paragraph 2

12. Ibid, paragraph 10

13. Ibid, paragraph 11

14. Ibid, paragraph 21

15. Bahá'u'lláh, *Súriy-i-Mulúk*, paragraph 12

16. *God Passes By*, p 185-186

17. Bahá'u'lláh, cited in *God Passes By*, p 188

18. Ibid, *The Kitáb-i-Aqdas*, paragraph 125

19. Ibid, paragraph 3

20. Ibid, paragraph 5

21. 'Abdu'l-Bahá, *Memorials of the Faithful*, chapter 8, 'Abdu's-Sálih, the Gardener

The Covenant

Bahá'u'lláh, the Prisoner, had overcome oppression. The innocent victim of every form of punishment, a prisoner in exile, He transformed His circumstances into spiritual and even material freedom. What's more, He gave us guidance to overcome oppression as well. He left writings and teachings to help us in our struggle against this monster. And most important, He established a Covenant that gives us a strong, reliable connection to the Creator. By holding fast to this connection we can absorb and redirect the force of those who seek to dominate us, and thus rise above oppression as well.

To understand how Bahá'u'lláh's Covenant releases us from oppression, we must first realize that oppression subverts our true nature, because it denies us free choice. As victims of an oppressive system, we are boxed in, pushed down, and have little or no say in our own destiny. Whether by force or manipulation, we are oppressed against our will. This goes against our nature, because we instinctively know and feel that we have been created with free will—with the right to make choices.

Of course, to form a society we have to give up some of our free will. When there are two of us, for example, the freedom for me to swing my fist ends at your nose, since you have the right to keep your nose intact. To preserve these rights, we make rules. As each member of the social group agrees to follow certain rules, she or he benefits, along with the group. To make these rules and protect the members' freedoms and rights, the group needs some kind of authority. If the authority is just and fair, most people will voluntarily accept to obey it, and the society can grow in harmony and good health.

In an oppressive system, however, the authority is tyranny, and the true nature of leadership becomes subverted. Instead of enforcing justice and protecting people's rights, a tyrant takes advantage of his position, and imposes unfair rules which the people are forced to obey. As the people try to rebel, revolt, or disobey, the tyrant crushes them, or manipulates them into fighting among themselves. The society's development gets frozen in power struggles and the people's true nature gets subverted.

What a loss. As human beings, we have enormous potential. With proper guidance and education, we can develop many noble qualities and discover divine attributes within ourselves and those around us. Seeing ourselves as spiritual beings, we naturally develop a desire to serve each other. Many of the people we admire most such as Mother Theresa, Albert Schweitzer, and Abraham Lincoln were those who served mankind in one way or another. Yet this natural impulse to serve is also subverted when people are forced to do it against their will. Involuntary service is nothing more than slavery—one of the most degrading forms of human existence, and one of the hallmarks of an oppressive system. Whether in the form of overt slavery, or as forced labor, indentured service, people's "collectives," child labor, or repetitive low-wage factory work, this kind of activity degrades human beings to the level of animals or machines.

A sad exhibit in the Montego Bay Cultural Centre portrays the daily life on Jamaica's slave plantations a few centuries ago. One particularly heartbreaking pen-and-ink drawing shows a mill used to crush sugar cane. The mill was powered by an enormous cylinder with wooden planks attached at regular intervals like the paddles of a wide water wheel. But instead of the weight of water, the power came from a row of slaves, hands chained above their heads, forced to climb a never-ending staircase of those planks. The sheer weight of their bodies and the energy it took to step up to each paddle of this treadmill provided the power needed to extract the cane juice.

This kind of oppression subverts our true nature. Neither the slave nor the slave owner achieves their full potential. To rise above the damaging effects of oppression and put it behind us once and for all, we need to reestablish our true nature. This means finding out who we really are, where we came from, and why we were created—our true purpose in life. A feeling that we were created for some purpose other than to be an animal or a machine will lead us eventually to try to make some kind of connection with our Creator. To help us in this endeavor, Bahá'u'lláh has given us guidance.

Spiritual Beings

Bahá'u'lláh says that although we are physically similar to animals in outward appearance, our true nature is spiritual. We were created to know and worship God. Our purpose in living is to develop spiritual qualities individually, and to create an ever-advancing civilization collectively. Bahá'u'lláh said that God created us through love, and that to benefit from that love, we must love God in return. The connection between ourselves and our Creator is a bond of love.

> O SON OF MAN! I loved thy creation, hence I created thee. Wherefore, do thou love Me, that I may name thy name and fill thy soul with the spirit of life.[1] - Bahá'u'lláh

This reciprocal bond of love between the Creator and ourselves is called, in religious terms, a Covenant. The Covenant is an agreement between mankind and its Creator, in which the Creator gives us certain blessings, but in order to receive them, we must follow certain guidelines. When we truly understand and experience the benefits of submitting to Divine authority, we willingly accept and abide by it. This is one way we show our love.

Since the Creator is beyond our physical experience, He sends a Messenger, a Representative. This Messenger appears as a human being who founds a religion and establishes the Covenant. Some scholars say the word "religion" originates with the Latin "religo," which means to re-tie, or reconnect.

Religion's purpose is to reconnect us to our Creator, or God. Each of the Founders of the world's major religions made a Covenant with Their followers, entrusted them with a Book for guidance, and promised Their return after some time. Although They appeared as men, They were in fact Manifestations of God on earth, true Representatives of the Creator.

> These Tabernacles of holiness, these primal Mirrors which reflect the light of unfading glory, are but expressions of Him Who is the Invisible of the Invisibles. By the revelation of these gems of divine virtue all the names and attributes of God, such as knowledge and power, sovereignty and dominion, mercy and wisdom, glory, bounty and grace, are made manifest.[2] - Bahá'u'lláh

From this perspective, the Covenant is established by an authority far greater than any king or president. As we have seen, Bahá'u'lláh wrote to the kings and rulers of the earth and told them of their duty to submit to God's authority. Those who ignored the Message soon found their kingdoms and empires in shambles. He also wrote to the Pope, the leaders of Islám, and to the priests and clergy of the world collectively. They generally ignored or opposed Him as well, and the world has since seen a steady decline in religious belief and in the ability of the clergy to control the minds of the people.

As for us, we too have the freedom to accept or reject the authority of Bahá'u'lláh as the Representative of the Creator. He wrote: "Whosoever desireth, let him turn aside from this counsel and whosoever desireth let him choose the path to his Lord."[3] Acceptance opens a clear path for us to follow, one that will ultimately free us from oppression. When we come to understand what Bahá'u'lláh is offering us, we want to follow the path, which eventually leads to voluntarily submitting to His authority. This path, this guidance, this authority is channeled and maintained in its purity and strength through the Covenant. It is this Covenant that has the power to loosen the knot of oppression.

> Today the pulsating power in the arteries of the body of the world is the spirit of the Covenant—the spirit which is the cause of life. Whosoever is vivified with this spirit, the freshness and beauty of life become manifest in him, he is baptized with the Holy Spirit, he is born again, is freed from oppression and tyranny, from heedlessness and harshness which deaden the spirit, and attains to everlasting life. [4] - 'Abdu'l-Bahá

In establishing this Covenant, Bahá'u'lláh created several ways to maintain our connection to the Creator after His passing. He set up two types of institutions—rulers and learned—to lead and guide us. The members of these institutions are chosen based on their knowledge of Bahá'u'lláh's teachings, and their devotion to Him. The rulers are elected to serve, administer and organize Bahá'í communities. The learned are appointed to give counsel and advice to the rulers and community members.

But before these institutions could function correctly, the believers had to be deepened in their Faith, and trained to administer it. To carry out these tasks, Bahá'u'lláh appointed his oldest son, 'Abdu'l-Bahá (which means "The Servant of Bahá"), as the Center of the Covenant, and made him responsible for leading the community and keeping it united. 'Abdu'l-Bahá in turn appointed his grandson, Shoghi Effendi, who continued working with the Bahá'ís to build and administer a world-wide community. Together these two individuals protected the Bahá'í community from divisions, and established the Covenant of Bahá'u'lláh on a firm foundation.

'Abdu'l-Bahá—The Center

We have made Thee a shelter for all mankind, a shield unto all who are in heaven and on earth, a stronghold for whosoever hath believed in God, the Incomparable, the All-Knowing. God grant that through Thee He may protect them, may enrich and sustain them, that He may inspire Thee with that which shall be a wellspring of wealth unto all created things, an ocean of bounty unto all men, and the dayspring of mercy unto all peoples.[5]
- Bahá'u'lláh

At the end of Bahá'u'lláh's earthly life, the Bahá'ís were left in a state of shock and sadness. They felt abandoned and forlorn. But Bahá'u'lláh had left them guidance in His books and writings. Now, they turned to a document called the Book of the Covenant. In that book Bahá'u'lláh explicitly appointed 'Abdu'l-Bahá as the Center of His Covenant, the person to whom all the Bahá'ís should turn for guidance upon His passing, the only authorized Interpreter of Bahá'u'lláh's life and writings.

'Abdu'l-Bahá's relationship to Bahá'u'lláh was special. He was born on May 23, 1844, the same day that the Báb declared His Mission to the First Letter of the Living. He was only nine years old when Bahá'u'lláh received His Revelation in the Síyáh-Chál, the Black Pit of Tehran. He lived with the exiles in Baghdád, and was the first person to become aware of His father's station as He Whom God will make Manifest, years before Bahá'u'lláh announced it in the Garden of Riḍván. On the long overland journey to Constantinople, 'Abdu'l-Bahá rode next to His father by day, and arranged for the comfort and food of the travelers at night. During the years of imprisonment in Adrianople and 'Akká He served as Bahá'u'lláh's representative for local government officials, townspeople, opponents and well-wishers, leaving Bahá'u'lláh free to meet with the believers, and to reveal the Sacred Writings. Now, upon Bahá'u'lláh's death, 'Abdu'l-Bahá was given the enormous responsibility to carry on the work of His father, and to keep the believers unified.

It was a most critical time for the Bahá'í Faith. Past religions at this point had become divided by confusion and conflict. With the Messenger gone, the followers disagreed about His purpose and the meaning of His Message. Whether with good intentions or selfish motives, they found themselves splitting into groups and sects based on their memories and interpretations of the Messenger's words. The ground was laid for power struggles that as the years and centuries passed have resulted in accusations, denunciations and separation into different denominations. One side's heroes were another side's heretics, and the fight was sometimes to the death. These divisions over interpretation continue right down to the present day, creating dozens of denominations and sects in every major religion, and generating ill-will among their members.

This has not happened in the Faith of Bahá'u'lláh, though. For the first time in religious history, the Messenger of God wrote down the message Himself at the time He revealed it. There can be no confusion about what was said, and no possibility for conflicting versions. Bahá'u'lláh left the equivalent of 100 volumes of writings, and these form the basis for His guidance. In addition to this protection, the writings provide for what the believers should do after His passing—namely turn to 'Abdu'l-Bahá for interpretation and further guidance.

As the appointed Interpreter of Bahá'u'lláh's life and writings, 'Abdu'l-Bahá formed a focal center around which the Bahá'ís could unite, and His life of service provided an example for them to follow. He wrote many letters to the Bahá'í communities then growing in Persia, 'Iráq, Turkey and the Holy Land, explaining to the Bahá'ís the spiritual truths found in Bahá'u'lláh's words, and answering their questions on different topics. He sent Bahá'í teachers to various parts of the world, including Europe and North America, and encouraged the growth of Bahá'í communities there.

Yet despite the clear instructions in the Book of the Covenant, some Bahá'ís, including members of Bahá'u'lláh's family, tried to discredit 'Abdu'l-Bahá, and claim leadership for themselves. This incessant desire for leadership has been another blight on the world's religions, leading to man-made hierarchies, concentrations of power, and ultimately, oppression. It comes from that part of our nature that wants to dominate and control others, and it must be suppressed if we are to advance as a society. 'Abdu'l-Bahá's brother, for example, grew jealous because he had not been appointed as the Center of Bahá'u'lláh's Covenant, and he did everything in his power to discredit 'Abdu'l-Bahá in the eyes of the believers and the government authorities.

A few other believers joined ranks with this man, and tried to create confusion and division among the Bahá'ís. They spread rumors and lies about 'Abdu'l-Bahá, saying that He was trying to start a rebellion against the Turkish Empire. As a result, 'Abdu'l-Bahá was re-confined in the city of 'Akká for several years, and even sentenced to death at one point.

They moved into and took over Bahá'u'lláh's mansion, stole His official seal and other possessions, and attempted to forge and alter His Writings, all to bolster their claim that they were the rightful followers.

Through it all, 'Abdu'l-Bahá showed sincere kindness and love towards these misguided souls, in the hope that they might see the error of their ways. But He did not allow them to cause any divisions in this new-born Faith. His ceaseless efforts preserved the unity of the Bahá'í Faith, making it the only religion in the world that has not divided into sects or denominations after the passing of its Founder. It would not be turned into a tool of oppression.

In 1909, as predicted by Bahá'u'lláh, the Sulṭán of Turkey was deposed, and 'Abdu'l-Bahá was released from prison. In 1912 He traveled to Europe and North America to visit the Bahá'ís there. He praised their faith and devotion to Bahá'u'lláh, and encouraged them to arise and serve. Although now in His late 60's and in poor health, He traveled by ship to New York and then by 3rd class train through the United States and Canada, giving over 130 formal talks, and holding many informal meetings with believers in 40 cities on both coasts and in the heartland. He returned via London, Paris, Stuttgart, Budapest, and Vienna, meeting with Bahá'ís and spiritual seekers in every place He stopped, giving them a glimpse of a new way of life.

In a talk in New York City 'Abdu'l-Bahá said:

Today the nations of the world are self-engaged, occupied with mortal and transitory accomplishments, consumed by the fires of passion and self. Self is dominant; enmity and animosity prevail. Nations and peoples are thinking only of their worldly interests and outcomes. The clash of war and din of strife are heard among them. But the friends of the Blessed Perfection (Bahá'u'lláh) have no thoughts save the thoughts of heaven and the love of God. Therefore, you must without delay employ your powers in spreading the effulgent glow of the love of God and so order your lives that you may be known and seen as examples of its radiance. You must deal with all in loving-kindness in order that this precious seed entrusted to your planting may continue to grow and bring forth its perfect fruit. The love and mercy of God will accomplish this through you if you have love in your own heart.[6]

For 'Abdu'l-Bahá, these were more than mere words. His life was an act of service, of sharing the love of God with all who met Him. He dressed modestly, spoke in a kindly and convincing way, gave generously of His money and possessions, listened intently to every person who spoke to Him, and looked lovingly upon each and all. He sought out the positive and could easily bring any conversation to a higher, more spiritual level. His every action was a lesson, not just for

The Covenant

those around Him, but when recorded and retold, for Bahá'ís in distant places and for generations to come.

As He was setting an example of how to live, 'Abdu'l-Bahá inspired the Bahá'ís to act. They, too, following His example, could arise and spread the Message of the Revelation of Bahá'u'lláh. To guide them in this endeavor, 'Abdu'l-Bahá wrote up a plan of action, and sent it in the form of letters to the Bahá'ís of the United States and Canada. There He laid out a broad plan to bring the Message of Bahá'u'lláh to the peoples of every country, territory, and island group in the world. These letters are known collectively as the Tablets of the Divine Plan.

During the final years of His life, 'Abdu'l-Bahá watched and encouraged various individuals who followed His example, transformed themselves spiritually, and traveled through their countries and around the world to share the guidance of Bahá'u'lláh. He wrote to them: "The full measure of your success is as yet unrevealed, its significance still unapprehended. Erelong ye will, with your own eyes, witness how brilliantly every one of you, even as a shining star, will radiate in the firmament of your country the light of divine Guidance, and will bestow upon its people the glory of an everlasting life."[7]

Shoghi Effendi—The Builder

In 1921 'Abdu'l-Bahá passed from this earthly life, and again the Bahá'ís were dismayed and saddened. Without the Center of the Covenant, it looked like the Faith might break apart and disintegrate. But 'Abdu'l-Bahá had left a will in which He appointed His grandson, Shoghi Effendi, as the Guardian of the Cause. This hereditary transfer of authority had been anticipated by Bahá'u'lláh in *The Most Holy Book*, and confirmed and explained in detail by 'Abdu'l-Bahá. The Guardian was to be the "expounder of the words of God" to whom all the Bahá'ís were to "show their obedience, submissiveness, and subordination."[8]

Shoghi Effendi was unique. He was a descendent of the families of both the Báb and Bahá'u'lláh. As a child he was small, sensitive, and very active. He grew up in 'Akká and Haifa, under the loving eye and guidance of his grandfather, 'Abdu'l-Bahá, to Whom he was completely devoted. He studied first at a Jesuit school in Haifa, then at a protestant school and college in Beirut. All the time he was away at school, he missed his beloved grandfather, and couldn't wait for school holidays when he could return to Him. Upon graduation in 1918, he started to work for 'Abdu'l-Bahá full time, assisting in administering to the needs of the Bahá'ís and the people of 'Akká. But two years later, 'Abdu'l-Bahá sent Shoghi Effendi to school again, this time to Oxford in England. Here the young man, among other things, deepened his knowledge and mastery of the English language. And it was here that he received the news of the passing of his dear grandfather.

Shoghi Effendi returned immediately to Haifa, and although just 24 years old at the time, this young man soon shouldered the full responsibility laid upon him by 'Abdu'l-Bahá, and began building. Based on the guidelines found in the writings of Bahá'u'lláh, and the outline of the Tablets of the Divine Plan and other writings of 'Abdu'l-Bahá, Shoghi Effendi went to work to construct a new world order.

A new world order requires a new pattern for social organization. This new pattern is not hierarchical like a pyramid, but is based on cooperation and consultation. The leaders in this new pattern are not found perched lazily at the top, giving orders and dictating commands to the followers below. Instead, they support the community at its base, acting as a foundation, consulting as a group, serving the needs of the community, and giving guidance based on their understanding of the authoritative words of Bahá'u'lláh, 'Abdu'l-Bahá, and now the Guardian. Leadership is not gained through dark intrigues and power struggles, nor through partisan politics and nominations. Administrators are elected by every adult member of the community, who base their choices on spiritual criteria.

This new style of functioning runs counter to the habits of thousands of years of oppression. Most of us aren't used to working cooperatively, or thinking of leadership as a position of service. Shoghi Effendi spent much of his life teaching the Bahá'ís how to follow this new pattern. As they learned, they began to function in a more united way. They elected Local Spiritual Assemblies. Following the guidance and instructions of the Guardian, these Assemblies began to learn a new way to administer a society based on love, unity, and divine authority; rather than domination, force, deceit, and a divide-and-rule mentality.

In addition to this guidance, Shoghi Effendi translated into English some of the major works of Bahá'u'lláh, and explained to the believers the importance of the respective roles of Bahá'u'lláh, the Báb, and 'Abdu'l-Bahá in the history of civilization. Based on this deeper knowledge and understanding, the Bahá'ís became more confident in teaching the Faith. As they taught and learned how to organize and administer their communities, the Guardian initiated a series of specific projects and plans to complement and fulfill the general goals laid out in the Tablets of the Divine Plan.

From the 1920s through the 1950s the Bahá'í community expanded from 35 to 254 countries (including territories, dependencies and colonies); its literature was translated into 237 languages, and over 197 different ethnic groups were represented. Today the Bahá'í Faith enjoys a world-wide following in excess of six million people, representing more than 2100 indigenous tribes, races and ethnic groups residing in more than 120,000 localities, in over 250 countries and independent territories around the world.[9]

The Covenant

When the Bahá'ís in a given country had formed Local Spiritual Assemblies in a sufficient number of communities, the Guardian allowed them to elect a National Spiritual Assembly. This institution is similar to a Local Assembly, but at the national level. Its nine members consult together and make decisions based on the writings of Bahá'u'lláh, 'Abdu'l-Bahá, and Shoghi Effendi.

Throughout Shoghi Effendi's Guardianship he faced relentless opposition from members of the families of Bahá'u'lláh and 'Abdu'l-Bahá, as well as a few other Bahá'ís they managed to influence. Although 'Abdu'l-Bahá's will left no room for doubt, these individuals saw a fresh opportunity to take control of the Faith now that 'Abdu'l-Bahá was gone and His young grandson had been put in charge.

By attacking the institutions of the Faith that had been established through the Covenant of Bahá'u'lláh, these people were more than simply misguided believers. Although they called themselves "Bahá'ís," they were knowingly and intentionally trying to destroy the Faith by attacking the Covenant. For this reason, when it became obvious that they were determined to continue their destructive behavior, both 'Abdu'l-Bahá in his time, and Shoghi Effendi in his, reluctantly named them "Covenant-breakers," and forbid the Bahá'ís to associate with them. Like protecting the body from a cancerous tissue, the prescribed remedy was surgical removal.

Some of the Covenant-breakers who had opposed 'Abdu'l-Bahá were still around at His passing. Another group formed from members of His family—His own children, mostly—as they grew jealous of this young grandson who had been given such responsibility. These people continued to occupy Bahá'u'lláh's home and attempted to control access to His nearby tomb, which was and still is considered a sacred shrine by the Bahá'ís. They stooped to new depths to discredit Shoghi Effendi and undermine his authority in whatever way they could. Over the years they tried to recruit followers among the Bahá'ís in Persia, 'Iráq, and the West. Although a few misguided believers did join them, the vast majority shunned them, and they never succeeded in breaking the unity of the Bahá'í Faith.

Predicting their ultimate downfall, 'Abdu'l-Bahá had written:

> These agitations of the violators are no more than the foam of the ocean, which is one of its inseparable features; but the ocean of the Covenant shall surge and shall cast ashore the bodies of the dead, for it cannot retain them. Thus it is seen that the ocean of the Covenant hath surged and surged until it hath thrown out the dead bodies—souls that are deprived of the Spirit of God and are lost in passion and self and are seeking leadership. This foam of the ocean shall not

endure and shall soon disperse and vanish, while the ocean of the Covenant shall eternally surge and roar. [10]

By the 1950s the Bahá'ís around the world had grown so firm in their faith, and so devoted to Shoghi Effendi, that the Covenant-breakers had ceased to be a threat. Most of them by now had seen all their schemes and ploys go sour and had lost the support of their few followers. Finally, in 1957, Shoghi Effendi was able to evict them from Bahá'u'lláh's house and the vicinity of His Shrine, and they soon faded from the scene.

The Learned and the Rulers

Bahá'u'lláh, 'Abdu'l-Bahá and Shoghi Effendi were not entirely alone in their work of building a new social order. As the Bahá'ís grew in their understanding of the Faith, they arose to help develop their communities. Some of the believers became so knowledgeable in Bahá'u'lláh's teachings, and so valuable in protecting the Covenant from attacks, that they were given a special designation—Hands of the Cause. The first Hands were appointed by Bahá'u'lláh, a few more by 'Abdu'l-Bahá, and then a substantial number by Shoghi Effendi, as the Faith spread over five continents. In addition to the Hands of the Cause, many other believers became distinguished scholars and teachers. This group of people collectively came to be known as the "learned" in the faith. Conjointly, members of the Local and National Spiritual Assemblies were referred to collectively as the "rulers."

The Hands of the Cause helped Shoghi Effendi by teaching and encouraging the Bahá'ís around the world, and by shouldering some of his growing administrative responsibilities in the Holy Land. They also helped him to protect the Cause against Covenant-breakers. One event they were not prepared for was the sudden death of Shoghi Effendi in 1957. Upon reading the Guardian's will, it was discovered that he had left no heir. He had been charged by 'Abdu'l-Bahá to appoint a hereditary successor who would be loyal and capable of leading the Bahá'í world, but the Guardian had had no children, nor was anyone in his family considered worthy, since they were mostly Covenant-breakers.

He had left a detailed plan of action, however—the Ten Year Crusade—that had begun in 1953 and would continue until 1963. And he was survived by 27 Hands of the Cause, who unanimously agreed to continue the implementation of the Ten Year Crusade, and at its conclusion, to hold the first election of the Universal House of Justice.

The Universal House of Justice is the supreme administrative body of the Bahá'í Faith. Its nine members are elected every five years by the members of every National Spiritual Assembly in the world. During the lifetime of Shoghi Effendi, it had not been possible to elect the Universal House of Justice, since he felt that the Bahá'ís were not spiritually mature enough, and there were not enough National Spiritual Assemblies to hold a proper election. But by 1963 there were 56 National Spiritual Assemblies in the world, and the Bahá'ís had reached a sufficient level of administrative experience and spiritual understanding to hold the election.

As the highest institution of the rulers, the Universal House of Justice was established by Bahá'u'lláh in *The Most Holy Book*. Its role was clarified by 'Abdu'l-Bahá and Shoghi Effendi, who explicitly stated that its decisions were divinely inspired and infallible. As such, it is a key element in the Covenant of Bahá'u'lláh. It performs a combination of legislative, executive, and judicial roles in that it gives guidance and enacts laws of the Faith, ensures that Bahá'u'lláh's teachings are understood and obeyed, and makes decisions on questions not specifically addressed in the writings of Bahá'u'lláh, 'Abdu'l-Bahá, or the Guardian. Thus it forms a vital link in the chain of guidance, maintaining a firm connection to the Creator that will continue unbroken as the Universal House of Justice continues to be elected, generation after generation.

Since it was not specifically authorized to appoint Hands of the Cause, one of the decisions of the Universal House of Justice was to create a new institution of the learned to carry on their function. This is called the Continental Board of Counselors. The Counselors are appointed by the Universal House of Justice to promote the teaching work of the Cause, and to protect its interests. They are assisted by Auxiliary Board members and their assistants at the national and local levels respectively.

Separation of Function

As the institutions of the learned and rulers expanded and developed, they were guided by a principle of separation of function. The rulers function always as consultative bodies, and are elected by the believers. Their job is to administer and coordinate Bahá'í community life. The learned on the other hand, function as individuals, and they are appointed to their positions. Their job is to encourage the believers and give advice and counsel to the rulers. Each institution has a clearly defined area of work, but all have the same goal: to uphold the Covenant and present the Message of Bahá'u'lláh to the peoples of the world. As their roles are different, Bahá'ís cannot serve as "rulers" and "learned" at the same time, except at the local level. This provides an important separation between leadership and scholarship that helps prevent the religion from disintegrating into just another oppressive system.

This separation, this balance between leadership and scholarship is unique to the Bahá'í Faith. In every previous religion, the tendency was to assume that the leader had the most knowledge of anyone. People accepted his authority on the assumption that he was either more divinely inspired than they, better read, or simply smarter. Those who disagreed with the leader's understanding of the Messenger or the Message were accused of defying authority. Authority in leadership was fused together with authority in scholarship. It was an all-or-nothing proposition. This concentration of power was partly to blame for the degradation of religious authority into oppressive tyranny.

The Covenant of Bahá'u'lláh removes this temptation, and it offers additional insight into a third, related element: power. Every oppressive system concentrates authority, knowledge, and power into the hands of a few people, or even just one person. The Covenant of Bahá'u'lláh keeps them apart. Authority is entrusted to the rulers. Specialization in knowledge is the area of the learned. And the power to act is found in each individual. It is the individual who provides initiative and energy to do the work, carry out the plans, and perform service. The individual accepts the role of Assembly member, Counselor, or Auxiliary Board Member—receiving neither salary nor special status. Without the power of the individual, who serves for love of Bahá'u'lláh, the institutions could not function.

You can think of the three elements: individuals, rulers, and learned like the parts of a sailing ship. The wind is the love of God, blowing freely. The individuals are the sails that catch the wind, providing power of movement. The rulers are the rudder that directs and guides the ship, and the learned are the compass and charts, that furnish the knowledge necessary to navigate. The rudder and compass are useless unless the ship is moving by the power of its sails. And what is the ship itself? It's the society, the community, that moves ahead when all the parts work together harmoniously.

Thus the Covenant of Bahá'u'lláh provides not only a way for us to connect with our Creator, but it establishes a foundation upon which we can build a new social order. We each have an important role to play. On the one hand we must transform ourselves as individuals, breaking free of thousands of years of oppressive history by strengthening our bond of love with the Creator. At the same time, we must also form bonds and ties of friendship and unity with each other, and learn to work together, so we can develop our society for the future. When these two types of connections are well-formed, we will find that the knot of oppression has simply vanished.

Notes

1. Bahá'u'lláh, *The Hidden Words of Bahá'u'lláh*, from the Arabic, number 4

2. Ibid, *The Kitáb-i-Íqán*, p 103

3. Ibid, *Bahá'í Prayers*, Tablet of Ahmad

4. 'Abdu'l-Bahá, *The Covenant*, extract 40

5. Bahá'u'lláh, cited in *The World Order of Bahá'u'lláh*, p 135-6

6. 'Abdu'l-Bahá, *The Promulgation of Universal Peace*, p 8

7. Ibid, *Tablets of the Divine Plan*, p 37

8. Ibid, *Will And Testament of 'Abdu'l-Bahá*, p 11

9. Statistics gleaned from:

Smith, Peter "The Bahá'í Faith: Distribution Statistics, 1925–1949" published in Journal of Religious History, Volume 39, issue 3, September 2015 https://onlinelibrary.wiley.com/doi/10.1111/1467-9809.12207

"Chronology of the Bábí and Bahá'í Faiths and related history" (an updated, expanded version of A Basic Baha'i Chronology by Glenn Cameron and Wendi Momen.) https://bahai-library.com/tags/Statistics

Bahá'í World News Service, "Media Information" https://news.bahai.org/media-information/statistics/

10. 'Abdu'l-Bahá, *Selections from the Writings of 'Abdu'l-Bahá*, pp 210-211

Personal Transformation

> O SON OF SPIRIT! Noble have I created thee, yet thou hast abased thyself. Rise then unto that for which thou wast created.[1] - Bahá'u'lláh

One of the more tragic results of oppression is the effect it has had on us as individuals. The model citizen in the current social order is a cow—an animal that simply consumes and produces—no questions asked. As long as you keep food in front of its face, you can take its milk. When it stops producing milk, you kill it. In our system, we accept the promise of the "good life"—a material paradise of consumer goods. As we consume more and more, we stimulate production, create more jobs and generate more profits for the wealthy elite. Some wealth eventually trickles down to the workers, and if they work hard and obey the rules, they too might get rich some day.

That's the theory. Unfortunately it overlooks an essential feature of human nature—the human heart. The heart gets lost in the process. On the one hand, the system stimulates greed, which reduces our capacity to love. On the other, if we are unable to produce or consume enough, we grow fearful and anxious. Either way, intense competition leads to anger, hostility and insensitivity to others. If we become aware of the plight of those less fortunate, we either feel guilty about our success, or we rationalize and tell ourselves that they deserve what they get. Many of us lose touch with our own feelings and get depressed. Whether through fear, anger, apathy or aloofness, we have learned to protect ourselves, closing ourselves off, closing our hearts.

Closed off and hurt, we look for some relief, and turn to the promise of material pleasure. We go shopping, to the movies, to the bars, the malls, or the great outdoors. We break speed limits and world records, conquer tall mountains or brave dangerous rapids. We plunge into our studies, work or hobbies, always looking for greater satisfaction. But the human heart has enormous capacity. It is difficult to satisfy. No matter how much we get, we still want more: more money, more power, a bigger car, a more beautiful house, a better sex partner. Even the super-rich can't seem to get enough to satisfy them. We look for love in every face, craving acceptance, nurturing, and affection wherever we can find it. But still it isn't enough. Why? Because the human heart has infinite capacity, a capacity so big that only the infinite love of the Creator can fill it. Until we find and receive this love, our hearts will remain empty and unsatisfied, and we will spend our lives trying to fill them.

Purifying the heart

> O SON OF DUST! All that is in heaven and earth I have ordained for thee, except the human heart, which I have made the habitation of My beauty and glory; yet thou didst give My home and dwelling to another than Me; and whenever the manifestation of My holiness sought His own abode, a stranger found He there....[2] - Bahá'u'lláh

Our heart belongs to the Creator. It's His home, and He is ready to occupy it. But it isn't ready for Him. It needs work. It's like someone's old garage—unused, closed up, dirty, and cluttered with useless junk. We have to break open the doors and clean out the garbage. We must correct our bad habits and sweep out the mundane desires and fancies that have taken us a lifetime to collect. This is the challenging process of personal transformation. It isn't easy, but the results are deeply satisfying. Bahá'u'lláh wrote:

> O SON OF SPIRIT! My first counsel is this: Possess a pure, kindly, and radiant heart, that thine may be a sovereignty ancient, imperishable, and everlasting.[3]

When our hearts are purified and overflowing with the love of our Creator, we will find ourselves immune to the devastating effects of oppression. We will discover we are capable of forgiving each other, of helping those less fortunate than ourselves, and of redirecting the pressure on us towards useful, healthy ends. Rather than resist, we will learn to acquiesce gracefully; rather than compete, we will learn to cooperate; rather than dominate, we will learn to lead by our example. We have the potential to do all these things and more, when our hearts are filled with the infinite love of the Creator.

Bahá'u'lláh has given us the means to purify our hearts — the creative Word of God. As the Messenger of God, Bahá'u'lláh has given us prayers that open our hearts to the healing balm of divine grace. He has revealed writings which help us meditate on our relationship to our Creator. He has renewed those spiritual laws we need in our efforts to live more in accord with God's Will. Each of His Writings is endowed with a special power to transform us.

> The Word of God is the king of words and its pervasive influence is incalculable. It hath ever dominated and will continue to dominate the realm of being. The Great Being saith: The Word is the master key for the whole world, inasmuch as through its potency the doors of the hearts of men, which in reality are the doors of heaven, are unlocked.[4] - Bahá'u'lláh

> Every word that proceedeth out of the mouth of God is endowed with such potency as can instill new life into every human frame, if ye be of them that comprehend this truth.[5] - Bahá'u'lláh

Personal Transformation

The words themselves have power. As we read them, they affect us. The mere act of reciting the Word of God helps bring that power alive.

> Whoso reciteth, in the privacy of his chamber, the verses revealed by God, the scattering angels of the Almighty shall scatter abroad the fragrance of the words uttered by his mouth, and shall cause the heart of every righteous man to throb. Though he may, at first, remain unaware of its effect, yet the virtue of the grace vouchsafed unto him must sooner or later exercise its influence upon his soul.[6] - Bahá'u'lláh

As our hearts become pure, we gain new capacity. We find ourselves more able to love, to forgive, and to help people. We also expand our capacity for deeper understanding of ourselves and our relationships with others. We grow thirsty for more knowledge, and turn to the Word of God more willingly for answers. With pure hearts, we are able to make better choices.

Making better choices

Making choices brings us to another essential feature of human nature—free will. Often in an oppressive environment, we feel as if we have lost our free will. We have no choice but to obey. We are blocked in by the tough facts of life, dominated by harsh taskmasters and pushed around by uncontrollable powers. But in every circumstance, no matter how difficult, we always have at least two options: to turn towards God, or to turn away.

This is the key to spiritual development. Turning towards God will lead us to right action, and will bring us to true happiness. Turning away from God leads to wrong action, and eventually to unhappiness. In whatever condition we find ourselves, whether in the lap of luxury or the pit of despair, we always have these two choices.

However, if our knowledge of God is somehow blocked, if we don't know which way to turn for guidance, we can quickly fall into the trap of wrong action. Perhaps the worst effect of oppression is that it can block our access to right knowledge. Without that guidance, it is virtually impossible to make those decisions that lead to happiness.

> What "oppression" is more grievous than that a soul seeking the truth, and wishing to attain unto the knowledge of God, should know not where to go for it and from whom to seek it?[7] - Bahá'u'lláh

Without the knowledge of God, we tend to follow our own ideas, often dictated by our ego or the world around us. As our heart is attached to material comforts, we lose sight of our spiritual destiny, and make wrong choices. These wrong choices lead to unhappiness. Our hearts become empty, and we desperately try to fill them with what we think they need. This leads to more wrong action, and more unhappiness. The result: we are truly oppressed.

With the knowledge of God, however, the vicious cycle is reversed. We begin to purify our hearts. As we purify our hearts, we grow more willing to accept Bahá'u'lláh's guidance, and more capable of choosing the right thing to do in a given situation. As we make more right choices, we grow happier. This happiness expands our heart, and gives us confidence. Our faith grows. We trust Bahá'u'lláh more, accept His guidance, take His Word more deeply into our hearts, and purify them even more. As the process continues we feel more and more free.

Tests

Thus we discover that it is not our material circumstances that oppress us. It is our access to the knowledge of God, and our willingness to accept and follow it. In fact, with this understanding we see how the material comforts and temptations of the "good life" can themselves lead to our oppression, if our hearts get caught up in them.

> O SON OF BEING! Busy not thyself with this world, for with fire We test the gold, and with gold We test Our servants.[8] - Bahá'u'lláh

No matter who we are, whether we live in luxury or poverty, whether we feel oppressed or not, we are being tested. If we pass the tests by choosing right action, we are rewarded by happiness. If we fail, choosing wrong action, we suffer. This is a spiritual law. Some call it the law of karma.

Good deeds bring joy to hearts; bad deeds bring suffering. But the law of karma isn't the only spiritual law. Sometimes we suffer through no fault of our own. Some people are born with physical handicaps or mentally deficient. Others lose one or both parents when they are young. Still others grow up in poverty, with little chance for decent food, clothes, or education. In our lives we all have accidents, misfortunes, and setbacks. Many of these are not our fault, but we still suffer as a result. This suffering is given to us by God, to test us, to help us discriminate between what is of lasting value, and what is relatively petty. 'Abdu'l-Bahá said:

> The mind and spirit of man advance when he is tried by suffering. The more the ground is ploughed the better the seed will grow, the better the harvest will be. Just as the plough furrows the earth deeply, purifying it of weeds and thistles, so suffering and tribulation free man from the petty affairs of this worldly life until he arrives at a state of complete detachment. His attitude in this world will be that of divine happiness. Man is, so to speak, unripe; the heat of the fire of suffering will mature him. Look back to the times past and you will find that the greatest men have suffered most.[9]

This deep spiritual truth about suffering has reassured many victims of oppression. It has sustained the peoples of tribes and nations who found themselves under the whip of the slave driver or boot of the tyrant. However, through unscrupulous manipulation, it has also become a tool in the arsenal of the tyrant. Promise people eternal rest and they will endure almost any hardship. Teach them about Jesus and they won't complain in the cotton fields. Give them a blessing from heaven and they will march off to battle. Assure them of paradise, and they will volunteer to become suicide bombers. Small wonder that religion has been stigmatized as the "opiate of the masses."

As we have seen, when the knowledge of God is lost or distorted, oppression fills the void, and we become the victims. But until we stop looking for someone to blame and start looking at our hardships as tests for our spiritual growth, we will never learn to take responsibility for our actions.

Taking responsibility

Being victimized by oppression, the temptation is to take the easy way out, to simply give up. Since we feel we have no free will or choice, and we are being forced into it, most of us cooperate. The problem is, whether we go along willingly or unwillingly, we lose a sense of responsibility for our actions. Like soldiers in an army, we just follow orders. Since those in charge take the credit for success, we also let them take the blame when things go wrong. Unfortunately, this habit carries over into our personal lives, and we get into the habit of blaming our circumstances and surroundings for our unhappiness. We blame our parents, our teachers, our friends, or our corrupt society for our failings. We look for any excuse, and try to find someone to take responsibility for us.

Thus we find a third element of human nature subverted by oppression: our ability to accept responsibility for our actions. Some societies have been oppressed for so long that they have incorporated this distortion of human nature into the very fabric of their culture. Formerly based on slave labor, these cultures have redefined and embraced the master-slave duality as a patron-client relationship, where the client renders obedience and service to the patron in exchange for favors and protection. The patron assumes full responsibility for the welfare of the clients, and makes all the important decisions for them. For lack of an alternative, the patron even becomes the client's role model.

In his book *Pedagogy of the Oppressed*, Paulo Freire describes this phenomenon as a duality within the heart of oppressed people. On the one hand, they desire freedom, but on the other hand, they fear it. They have internalized the consciousness of the oppressor, and to become free they must now become actors, rather than remain spectators. They have to speak out rather than keep silent. They must begin to exercise their creative power to transform the world.

Although the client-patron system may seem convenient, it's a trap that's difficult to escape. It tempts us to avoid responsibility with a false promise of security. It saps our self-confidence and initiative to act and work independently.

Personal Transformation

We deserve more. Every human being is a unique creature of God, with unlimited potential. We deserve a chance to realize that potential, to grow and develop ourselves into truly noble beings. Part of that growth means making choices, and taking responsibility for the result. As each of us works to realize our full potential, we will be able to contribute enormously to rebuilding our society.

The document *The Prosperity of Humankind*, written at the request of the Universal House of Justice, states, "The long, slow civilizing of human character has been a sporadic development, uneven and admittedly inequitable in the material advantages it has conferred. Nevertheless, endowed with the wealth of all the genetic and cultural diversity that has evolved through past ages, the earth's inhabitants are now challenged to draw on their collective inheritance to take up, consciously and systematically, the responsibility for the design of their future."[10]

We are the ones who must take up this responsibility. In the past we might have looked around expecting someone more powerful, more wise, or more capable to do the job. But now, at this time in our history, we are responsible for our destiny. We have the capacity. All we need is the will to move forward.

> Unto each one hath been prescribed a preordained measure, as decreed in God's mighty and guarded Tablets. All that which ye potentially possess can,

however, be manifested only as a result of your own volition.[11] - Bahá'u'lláh

Our actions are our witnesses. The level of progress or perversion of our nature can easily be seen in what we do. With hearts closed up and hurt, lacking knowledge of God, making wrong choices and refusing responsibility for the outcome, we find ourselves destroying each other and our environment, pushing our society and civilization ever faster down the road to self-annihilation. On the other hand, with pure, radiant hearts, filled with the love and knowledge of God, choosing to follow His guidance and taking responsibility for ourselves, we stand ready to contribute to our society. We are ready to serve.

Service

Perhaps the least-understood element of human nature in an oppressive regime is service. Although the servant has traditionally been considered the lowest level in the social order, Bahá'u'lláh tells us that service is the one of the noblest expressions of humanity:

> Man's merit lieth in service and virtue and not in the pageantry of wealth and riches.[12]

This is tough to accept. Finally, after getting a glimpse of a life of freedom, of spiritual loftiness, of soaring in the heavens of love and knowledge, now we have to do what? To serve?

Like wash dishes? Clean toilets? Take out the garbage? Do you mean to say we have to visit our sick neighbor, volunteer for community service, and give blood? Yes, that's part of it. But there's more. There's fighting fires, policing the streets, and delivering the mail. There's teaching children, tending to the sick, and raising plants and animals for food. Someone has to manufacture, distribute and sell clothes, dishes, furniture and appliances. Others work in transportation, communications and power utilities. We all have work to do. We all have to live in this world.

We have to be in this world, but we don't have to be of this world. It's all a question of attitude, of motive. If we work just for money, just to survive, just to get rich and satisfy our material cravings, we'll never be truly happy, and we probably won't do our best. However, if we understand that our work is service to humanity, and that through working we are worshiping God, things are different. As we grow in our love and understanding of our Creator, we discover one of the reasons we were created—to serve. We find that in whatever job we do, we are serving someone.

> All humanity must obtain a livelihood by sweat of the brow and bodily exertion, at the same time seeking to lift the burden of others, striving to be the source of comfort to souls and facilitating the means of living. This in itself is devotion to God. Bahá'u'lláh has thereby encouraged action and stimulated service. But the

energies of the heart must not be attached to these things; the soul must not be completely occupied with them. Though the mind is busy, the heart must be attracted toward the Kingdom of God in order that the virtues of humanity may be attained from every direction and source.[13] - 'Abdu'l-Bahá

Imagine a society where people's primary motive for working was to serve their fellow humans and to serve God. Of course we would still receive incomes, but what a difference in our lives and attitudes! What care we would take to do things right. What devotion and love we would put into every action. What appreciation we would feel for our fellow workers. Each of us would be treated like kings and royalty, and yet each of us would be servants. Working side by side, in harmony, our hearts filled with the love and knowledge of our Creator, striving day by day to make better choices, to learn to submit our will to His Will, taking responsibility for our lives, we would find ourselves living in paradise.

Achieving this dream calls for personal transformation. But that's not all. As each of us transforms ourselves, we also have to improve our interactions, our relationships, our social order. We have to break out of the old, oppressive ways of treating each other, and discover new ways of working and living together. Then we will see the knot of oppression disappear altogether, never to return.

Notes

1. Bahá'u'lláh, *The Hidden Words of Bahá'u'lláh*, from the Arabic, number 22
2. Ibid, from the Persian, number 27
3. Ibid, from the Arabic, number 1
4. Bahá'u'lláh, *Tablets of Bahá'u'lláh*, p 173
5. Ibid, *Gleanings from the Writings of Bahá'u'lláh*, LXXIV
6. Ibid, CXXXVI
7. Bahá'u'lláh, *The Kitáb-i-Íqán*, p 31
8. Ibid, *The Hidden Words of Bahá'u'lláh*, from the Arabic, number 55
9. 'Abdu'l-Bahá, *Paris Talks*, p 178
10. *The Prosperity of Humankind*, paragraph 3
11. Bahá'u'lláh, *Gleanings from the Writings of Bahá'u'lláh*, LXXVII
12. Ibid, *Tablets of Bahá'u'lláh*, p 138
13. 'Abdu'l-Bahá, *The Promulgation of Universal Peace*, p 187

Social Development

We've now come to the very heart of the issue: How to develop a new kind of society? Personal transformation is an important step, but unless we have a new social structure, people could all too easily slip back into habits of oppression.

It has happened in the past. Each Messenger of God brought the means for personal transformation. Many devout believers followed the guidance, and achieved remarkable spiritual progress. But the framework of an oppressive system remained. As certain individuals lusted after leadership and power the religions lost their purpose and much of their transformative potential. Some sects and denominations have become irrelevant and weak, others fanatical or oppressive. Around the world today we can see the results—the coolness of apathy and atheism alternating with fires of hatred and war that burn in the name of religion.

But now we have a chance to move past those pitfalls. We've seen how Bahá'u'lláh has given us a Covenant to protect against the misinterpretation of His teachings. And we've seen how we can transform ourselves through His Word. Now we need to understand and apply His social teachings, because they offer us a way to develop a new kind of society based on justice and unity.

The purpose of Bahá'u'lláh's coming, the main point of His Message, the central theme of His Revelation, is unity. He said that humanity has reached a point in its development where it must come together, to be as one family, like the branches of one tree or the waves of one ocean. He said there is only one God, that all the religions come from that one God, and that mankind was created by that one God. Now is the time for us to understand and manifest this oneness, to be reunited into one human race.

Creating Unity

The utterance of God is a lamp, whose light is these words: Ye are the fruits of one tree, and the leaves of one branch. Deal ye one with another with the utmost love and harmony, with friendliness and fellowship. He Who is the Day Star of Truth beareth Me witness! So powerful is the light of unity that it can illuminate the whole earth.[1] - Bahá'u'lláh

How can we possibly unite the human race? We have to start at home, next door, at work and at school. As we transform ourselves and open our hearts to the infinite love of the Creator, we find that this love has to move. It has to flow. It reaches out to others, and embraces them. We find ourselves making new acquaintances, new friends, new bonds of love and unity. If we really want to build a new society, we have to love and trust each other; we have to weave bonds of love and fellowship. There is no alternative.

The opposite of unity, and one of the hallmarks of oppression, is division. Those who would dominate seek to divide: through telling little lies, keeping secrets, promising special privileges, encouraging distrust and misunderstandings, creating hierarchies, promoting prejudices, feeding racist tendencies, and deepening fears. The oppressor relies on our lower human nature to magnify our differences, enlarge any divisions, create competition, and start fights, always directing our anger and resentment at each other instead of him, while he watches us grow weak and powerless. Once a crack starts, if we aren't careful, it quickly grows longer and wider. If not repaired, it generates more cracks and fissures, and soon the whole surface breaks up and collapses. Bahá'u'lláh warns us:

> Beware lest the desires of the flesh and of a corrupt inclination provoke divisions among you. Be ye as the fingers of one hand, the members of one body.[2]

One way to think about the unity of the human race is to picture each one of us as cells in the body of mankind. Each cell is alive, each is unique. Each has an important role to play in the life of the body, and they must work together. Millions of cells, united together, form structures and organs. Bone cells support the body. Muscle cells move its arms and legs. Stomach and intestinal cells help digest food. Blood cells transport nourishment and waste products. Brain and nerve cells receive stimuli and coordinate responses. Some of these functions may seem more glamorous or important, but all are necessary. Each organ of the body, each group of tissues, every cell, plays a role.

In the same way, each of us has a role to play in society. Each of us is different, and as we each contribute our unique talents and abilities, our society benefits. However, we have to work together harmoniously, to coordinate our efforts. If one group of cells in the body functions out of harmony, the result is sickness. A cancerous tissue drains the nutrients of the other cells to feed its own unnecessary growth. If the cancer isn't removed, the whole body dies, and the cancer cells die with it. Likewise, when one group of people seeks to dominate others for their own advantage, everyone suffers, including those who dominate.

Authority

What we need is some kind of organization, which will require self-regulation and self-control. The cells of the body function more or less automatically, according to their nature encoded in DNA. We, on the other hand, have free choice. We have to decide to come together. We have to choose to create a society. We have to voluntarily accept some kind of authority or control, realizing that if we don't, the whole society will fall apart, and we will all suffer.

This authority, however, has to be just. It must be fair. It should regulate and balance our activities and efforts in such a way that each person develops their full potential, maximizes their opportunities, contributes fully, and receives adequate material support. The authority should allocate resources for maximum benefit. It should consider the needs of each individual, be they of the majority or minority. It should encourage diversity and individual initiative, guiding and directing their expression in ever more profound levels of unity.

This sounds wonderful, perhaps even idealistic, considering our history. We haven't seen this kind of authority very often, neither in national or local politics, nor between nations. We're more used to hearing these ideals spoken out, but seeing instead competition, political corruption, favoritism and petty tyranny. Many of these problems stem from a limited number of choices in the type of authority. Most social structures are based on one of two general alternatives: dictatorial or adversarial. Each has its advantages, but both ultimately lead to disunity and injustice. Let's take a closer look.

A dictatorship, or one-person rule, has the advantage of expediency. Decisions are made quickly. The orders are given and carried out. Everyone follows, or is punished. In classic pyramid-like fashion, the society maintains its structure. But there is a fatal flaw—the intense concentration of power and responsibility is virtually impossible to bear. For those few dictators who have chosen to be benevolent, organizing and running a society based on justice and fairness proved to be an enormous challenge. Small wonder that most of history's despots have chosen the easier path—to make life as comfortable as possible for themselves, and let the people bear the burden. The obvious response to this manifest injustice is to rebel. To stay in control, the dictator resorts to the tools and methods of oppression, manipulating and dividing the people. The final result of most dictatorships is thus injustice and disunity.

To counteract this human temptation for power, we have conceived another type of system—partisanship. Here, several individuals or groups compete against each other for leadership. The people vote, and the majority rules. This way, in theory, at least most of the people are satisfied. However, since the minority is not satisfied, they continually challenge the majority and the status quo. The system grants them this right, which serves as a check against despotic excesses. Even in uncorrupted democracy the division and competition between the groups creates an adversarial climate, ultimately leading to disunity. Justice is done in favor of those who present the best argument, who can make the best case. But is that really justice?

What is justice, exactly? The word conjures up images of courtrooms, judges, attorneys and juries. Under a dictatorial system, one person decides the case. You might get lucky and be judged by a Solomon, but the chances aren't too good.

Under an adversarial system, at least there are two sides—the prosecution and the defense. Here we achieve some sort of balance, as each side presents those facts which favor the accuser or the accused. It is certainly more balanced than the arbitrary decisions and rule of a despot, but is it the best possible way?

An inherent flaw is this simple fact: conflict conceals truth. As each side presents their case, they do so with the intent of winning. The prosecution skillfully brings to light all the possible evidence to show the accused is guilty, and tries to conceal any facts to the contrary. The defense tries to paint the opposite picture. The judge or jury have to decide which of these stories is the truth. In fact, because of adversarial pressure, both sides are necessarily distorted. The truth is rarely black or white; most of the time it is found to hold many shades of color.

Justice is concerned with finding the truth. When the truth is brought to light, fair and equitable solutions can be found. Discovering the truth, and coming up with creative solutions that are fair and just is a challenging process. It requires a clear mind and an unbiased heart. Decision-makers must let go of their preconceived notions, think deeply, and apply the laws at their most profound level. Unfortunately, an adversarial climate restricts this ability. In an atmosphere of contention and hostility people get confused by conflicting statements, swayed by emotional appeals, and convinced by exaggerated and misleading oratory. They make decisions based on superficial reasons, and often the truth never really comes to light. If we want to get to the truth, to administer justice and evolve toward some kind of authority that everyone is willing to trust, we need a better way of making decisions. For this purpose, Bahá'u'lláh has given us a tool: consultation.

Consultation

> The Great Being saith: The heaven of divine wisdom is illumined with the two luminaries of consultation and compassion. Take ye counsel together in all matters, inasmuch as consultation is the lamp of guidance which leadeth the way, and is the bestower of understanding.[3]
> - Bahá'u'lláh

Consultation is a powerful tool for dismantling the effects of oppression. It can be used at any level, in any size of social group, even as few as two. It is for wives and husbands, families and friends, committee members, business associates, project planners, youth groups, and administrative teams. It effectively addresses any kind of question, problem, conflict, or opportunity. It is a way to make decisions by tapping the creative genius of every member of the group, often leading to extraordinary solutions that no one had originally conceived of. Consultation brings together differing viewpoints of reality, each offering a unique perspective, each containing part of the truth. It uncovers those common elements that express the truth in a way that no single participant could have envisioned alone. When consultation is conducted properly, it offers the best guidance that a group of people can hope to receive. Done well, consulting is an art and a science, a continuously evolving discovery of how to think and work together. When we learn how to consult, we bring new light to our daily affairs. When our leaders learn how to consult, we will have a basis for equality and justice in our society.

But it must be done correctly, according to the instructions laid out by 'Abdu'l-Bahá. If not, we will fall back into our old habits, and lose out on the benefits. Proper consultation requires certain initial conditions, the correct attitudes, and the following of a few clear steps. These may appear simple enough, but they demand a complete change in orientation from everything most of us are used to. For example, we must establish love and harmony among ourselves, turn our hearts to God, express ourselves with courtesy, dignity and moderation, respect the views of others, not jump to conclusions, and most important, not insist on our own opinions. The success we achieve in consultation depends on our level of personal development. This being the case, you might think that there is no point in attempting to consult if we haven't progressed very far in our efforts at personal transformation. In one sense, that's true, but consultation can be a transformative process in itself. If we enter into consultation with a sincere interest to do our best, we will find many opportunities to grow spiritually. As with personal transformation, the process may be painful at times, but the rewards are worth it.

There are five general parts to consultation. First, the facts of the situation must be presented. These could come from various sources, including group members, witnesses, outside experts, reference materials, and so on. Next, any principles or laws that might bear on the issue must be introduced. Of course, the source of this guidance would depend on the circumstances of the situation. Third, with the facts and principles before them, the members of the group then engage in free discussion. Each person has the right and obligation to speak and give their views. Each has the duty to listen and consider the opinion of others. The views thus expressed become the property of the group as a whole. As such, they can be questioned, challenged, and modified as necessary. This process of working with ideas and proposals is the heart of consultation. At some point, if the group is working together harmoniously towards a common goal, an idea or possible solution begins to take shape. It usually reflects the input of many people, and it is often an entirely new creation, an unexpected outcome. This is the time to make a decision, the fourth part of consultation. Ideally, and in most cases, the decision will be unanimous. It might become necessary to take a vote, though. If the majority is in favor of the decision, it passes. After a decision is made comes the fifth and final part of consultation—action. The process isn't complete until action is taken. This action must be united, with every member of the group participating wholeheartedly. Even those who did not vote in favor must support the decision once it is made. The essential guideline is unity—unity in thought and action. Thus in consultation we discover a way to unite ourselves, to coordinate our activity, and to administer justice in our society.

> Man must consult on all matters, whether major or minor, so that he may become cognizant of what is good. Consultation giveth him insight into things and enableth him to delve into questions which are unknown. The light of truth shineth from the faces of those who engage in consultation. Such consultation causeth the living waters to flow in the meadows of man's reality, the rays of ancient glory to shine upon him, and the tree of his being to be adorned with wondrous fruit. The members who are consulting, however, should behave in the utmost love, harmony and sincerity towards each other. The principle of consultation is one of the most fundamental elements of the divine edifice. Even in their ordinary affairs the individual members of society should consult.[4] - 'Abdu'l-Bahá

This principle of consultation gives us hope for fair and effective leadership. It provides a powerful force for justice, particularly in administrative systems. We've already seen how the administrative institutions of the Bahá'í Faith were created and are guided by Bahá'u'lláh through His Covenant, how they are elected by secret ballot, with no adversarial parties or politics, and how they put service to God and humanity as their highest ambition. Now we see how, by consulting together, the members of Spiritual Assemblies can work together to lead their respective communities. They can make fair, impartial decisions for the benefit of the whole group, guiding the community based on profound understanding and application of the writings of Bahá'u'lláh, 'Abdu'l-Bahá, Shoghi Effendi, and the Universal House of Justice. As Assembly members grow in their understanding and love for the Creator, they improve their ability to consult, and thus grow ever more perfect in their ability to serve and administer to the needs of the community.

Obedience

This kind of administration is a fundamental foundation for a new society. But there is another side to the administrative equation—obedience. For our society to function well, we must obey the rules, a big challenge for all of us. We share an oppressive heritage, where authority is suspect to say the least, if not questioned, challenged, and sometimes completely rejected. Those habits were formed from experiences of thousands of years of tyrannical, oppressive rule. We have learned our lessons well—how to resist, to challenge, to evade, and to shrug off authority.

Now, as we freely elect our administrators from the best among ourselves, respecting their wisdom, selflessness, servitude to humanity and devotion to God, we in turn must submit to their authority and obey them. For everyone's benefit, we all must follow their rules and abide by their decisions. Within the Bahá'í framework there are avenues provided for legitimate complaints, appeals, and questions. But the guideline is to obey first and appeal later.

> It is incumbent upon everyone not to take any step without consulting the Spiritual Assembly, and they must assuredly obey with heart and soul its bidding and be submissive unto it, that things may be properly ordered and well arranged.[5] - 'Abdu'l-Bahá

This principle of obedience will bring order to the increasing chaos of society, but an order based on divine love and knowledge, rather than force and coercion. In the past we obeyed only grudgingly, forced into compliance by tyrannical forces. When we found the laws to be unfair, we felt justified in breaking them. Revolt and revolution were obvious responses. So were lying, cheating, and stealing from those in power. The final result was either chaos or still greater oppression, or both.

But now we have to change our habits. As we see our administrators working on our behalf, consulting together, voluntarily giving up their time for the community's benefit, striving to put spiritual laws and principles into practice, we get inspired. We grow more willing to set aside our differences and to give up some of our selfish interests. Also, as we grow in our ability to follow the guidance of Bahá'u'lláh and transform our lives with His Word, we begin to understand the benefits to ourselves of obeying His institutions. And as we obey, we find ourselves even more capable of making right choices and taking responsibility for them. We become even happier.

And here's an ironic twist: as we obey we become leaders. In this new social order, as we follow the guidance of Bahá'u'lláh and the institutions of His Covenant, we transform ourselves, and set an example for others to follow. We grow more loving, trustworthy, caring, honest, responsible, devoted, helpful, and filled with many other divine virtues. We feel a new happiness surging within us, and naturally want to share it. We tell other people about what we have found, and how it has transformed us. They may or may not believe our words, but they can't deny our actions. When we treat them with patience, respect, humor and courtesy, they respond in kind. We teach them the truths we have discovered through our example. In our lives, through our actions, we become leaders.

> O SON OF MY HANDMAID! Guidance hath ever been given by words, and now it is given by deeds. Everyone must show forth deeds that are pure and holy, for words

are the property of all alike, whereas such deeds as these belong only to Our loved ones. Strive then with heart and soul to distinguish yourselves by your deeds. In this wise We counsel you in this holy and resplendent tablet.[6] - Bahá'u'lláh

The old, destructive, lose-lose habits of competition for leadership and position in the hierarchy turn into a win-win competition to acquire virtues and to serve each other. Each person in society has the opportunity to be a leader. At the same time, each is also a follower. Those who follow best become the best leaders. Whether in a position of authority and administration or not, whether serving on an institution of rulers or learned or not, we all have a chance to lead. The field of moral leadership is wide open. The better we lead, the more we inspire others to lead. Soon we find ourselves in a spiritual school where every student is a teacher and every teacher a student. We work in a company where everyone serves everyone else. We live in a society where all support each other, and no one is put down or left out. We create unity.

> With the utmost unity, and in a spirit of perfect fellowship, exert yourselves, that ye may be enabled to achieve that which beseemeth this Day of God.[7] - Bahá'u'lláh

Notes

1. Bahá'u'lláh, *Gleanings from the Writings of Bahá'u'lláh*, CXXXII

2. Ibid, *The Kitáb-i-Aqdas*, paragraph 58

3. Ibid, *Tablets of Bahá'u'lláh*, p 168

4. 'Abdu'l-Bahá, *Consultation: A Compilation*, extract 14

5. Ibid, extract 8

6. Bahá'u'lláh, *The Hidden Words of Bahá'u'lláh*, from the Persian, number 76

7. Ibid, *Gleanings from the Writings of Bahá'u'lláh*, XCVI

Paradigm Shift

Hold an orange seed in your hand. How does it feel? Small, dry, and hard. Not much to consider, really. Looking at the seed, it's difficult to imagine that a whole tree could grow out of it. But it can. If you put the seed in a moist place, and keep it warm, an interesting thing starts to happen. It starts to swell up, to expand a little. The hard shell gets a little softer. The seed swells up more and more until finally the shell breaks. Out comes a little shoot—the first sign of life. The shell falls off and disintegrates, but if the shoot has soil, water, and sunlight, it grows. It puts out roots, leaves, and branches. It grows strong and tall, giving fruit. Inside each orange—more seeds.

The orange seed is an expression of intelligence. It contains the instructions (in the form of DNA) and nutrients necessary to start the growth of an orange tree. What's more, this intelligence is well packaged and preserved; seeds from oranges and other kinds of plants have been known to germinate and grow after many years. The shell casing is hard, protecting the seed until the conditions are right for growth. If you break the shell, the seed will soon spoil, and cannot grow.

The tree is also an expression of intelligence. The DNA instructions of the seed become manifest in the tree, and we can see its green color and beautiful form. We can pick the oranges and eat them. The tree isn't so well protected as the seed; its leaves and branches are far more vulnerable, and it depends on sunlight, water, and soil. But it is alive.

In the seed and the tree you have two types of intelligence, two types of perfection—one is inert and the other is alive. Both are stable, but one shows static stability, the other dynamic stability. Which is better? That depends on the circumstances. Both are necessary; each has its place in nature. What is of interest to us is how the seed changes from its inert level of perfection to its dynamic level, because a similar process is currently taking place in our society.

Right now human society is in the midst of a paradigm shift. It is the biggest change in civilization in recorded history. Although many people aren't aware of it, all of us feel the effects. The seed of our society has germinated, and the hard shell of oppression is softening and cracking open. As it does, we see a new creation emerge.

Features of a paradigm shift

Although this sounds pretty dramatic, paradigm shifts are common in nature, and they all follow the same basic pattern. A paradigm shift starts with a certain stability, a relatively low level of order—that's the original paradigm. Then comes some kind of outside influence or energy that puts pressure on the system, causing change, turbulence, or chaos within it. Into this chaotic environment, a pure, orderly element is introduced. This pure element channels the new energy in the system, permeating the chaos with order, causing a rapid shift in organization that leads to a higher, more complex level of stability. This new level of stability is the new paradigm.

There are lots of examples of paradigm shifts in the world of nature. Consider silicon atoms. They are commonly found in nature, such as in beach sand, which is useful for making concrete, but is not particularly valuable. When you take this same silicon and heat it, the atoms move about quickly and chaotically as the substance melts. At this point, you introduce a small but perfect seed crystal—silicon atoms arranged in perfect order. If the molten silicon cools in just the right way, its atoms arrange themselves around the crystal in the same perfect pattern, creating a very large silicon crystal. This stable crystal structure embodies a higher amount of order and intelligence than common beach sand, so much so that it can be used to make computer chips.

Consider a pot of cooking oil. At room temperature, the oil sits in a static stable state. If you put a flame under the pot, the oil molecules near the flame get hot and start to move faster. Some of them move away from the heat, into areas where the molecules are cooler, moving slower. They agitate those molecules, making them move faster. At first the situation is chaotic as faster moving molecules keep bumping into slower moving ones. But then, suddenly, the whole system transforms itself into a rolling convection current. The heated molecules move up, away from the flame, to the top of the pot, where they spread out, cool off, and travel down the sides of the pot, back to the flame. As long as the flame is on, the circulation process continues, and the system maintains this higher level of order, this dynamic stability.

Let's look at the plant and animal kingdoms. Recent discoveries in the study of the theory of evolution show how a certain species will maintain its characteristics for many thousands of years as long as the environment is stable. If, however, a new influence or stimulus, such as a natural disaster or climate change, puts undue pressure on the environment, the plants or animals will respond by producing many mutations in their DNA, causing notable variations in types of offspring. A few of these new members of the species are best adapted to the new conditions. They will tend to survive, replicate, and flourish, so that within a few generations the entire species has evolved to a new level.

In these examples, a paradigm shift is a spontaneous response of the system to external pressure. The inherent intelligence of the system is stimulated, and through a transformative process it becomes manifest in a higher level of order. The beauty of the silicon crystal, the orderly motion of the oil molecules, and the new plant or animal species are all manifest expressions of intelligence. This intelligence was always there within the system, and is simply "forced" out into the open by changing circumstances.

A New Social Paradigm

People in different parts of the world are starting to look at this paradigm shift idea as a model for the chaotic change we are experiencing in society. Most of us are aware that we are living in a very turbulent time in history filled with rapid change, growth, and disintegration. The old, familiar, stable way of life is falling apart. All around us we can see the destruction of the existing paradigm of social order. Many familiar institutions are breaking down or losing importance—the family, the church, the government. We see an explosion of chaos and creativity in the arts. The pace of our lives is accelerating daily from new technologies and ever-faster means of communication. It's as if some invisible force is moving through our lives, compelling us to move faster, higher, and farther than ever before.

This force, this energy is coming from the Revelation of Bahá'u'lláh. Unseen and for the most part, unnoticed, our Creator is working in the world. The seed of human society has germinated, and is swelling up. Soon we will see it break out of the hard shell that has surrounded it for centuries and put out fresh green shoots of a new civilization.

> The world's equilibrium hath been upset through the vibrating influence of this most great, this new World Order. Mankind's ordered life hath been revolutionized through the agency of this unique, this wondrous

System—the like of which mortal eyes have never witnessed.[1] - Bahá'u'lláh

The seed is swelling and swelling. Soon it has to burst open. When? We don't know exactly. It has been swelling up for almost two centuries, since the announcement of the Báb in 1844. We've seen lots of changes in the world since that time, a lot of material progress, and a lot of human suffering. Most thinking people in the world today agree that we cannot continue down the path we are racing for much longer. Sooner or later, be it through overpopulation, climate change, world-wide epidemics, financial collapse or another global war, we're going to hit a brick wall.

> The world is in travail, and its agitation waxeth day by day. Its face is turned towards waywardness and unbelief. Such shall be its plight, that to disclose it now would not be meet and seemly. Its perversity will long continue. And when the appointed hour is come, there shall suddenly appear that which shall cause the limbs of mankind to quake. Then, and only then, will the Divine Standard be unfurled, and the Nightingale of Paradise warble its melody.[2] - Bahá'u'lláh

We will reach a point where there will be a sudden turn of events. In every paradigm shift, after all the necessary elements are in place, there comes one defining moment, one critical instant where the system experiences maximum stress. At that point a small but well organized variable on the periphery of the system exerts a disproportionately strong influence, and in relatively short time creates a new paradigm.

> The Call of God, when raised, breathed a new life into the body of mankind, and infused a new spirit into the whole creation. It is for this reason that the world hath been moved to its depths, and the hearts and consciences of men been quickened. Erelong the evidences of this regeneration will be revealed, and the fast asleep will be awakened.[3] - 'Abdu'l-Bahá

This "Call of God" is our stimulus for the new paradigm. As we hear the call and wake up, we feel a new energy coursing through ourselves and society. We want to respond, to move, to join the cosmic dance, but we don't know the steps. We want to do our part, to break free of oppression, and build a new world. But we need help. Without help we can only try to channel this new energy into the social models, the pyramids, that have shaped our civilization for thousands of years. And yet all around us we see the pyramids crumbling, disintegrating under the power of this new, divine energy.

Guidance and Vision

We don't have to try so hard. The "Call of God" is self-contained. As well as energy it brings guidance—guidance to rebuild our lives and our world. The water and sunlight on the orange seed cause it to break out of its shell, but this same water and sunlight also provide necessary nourishment for the seed to grow into a tree. In like manner, the energy released by Bahá'u'lláh that has upset the world's equilibrium and revolutionized our ordered life has also endowed us with a new spiritual capacity to rebuild our society. What's more, it comes complete with all the guidance we need.

One source of guidance is the Word of God, which provides an authentic, permanent, written record of the teachings and laws that will restructure our society, revealed in a form that breathes spirit and life into whoever reads them.

> This is a Book which hath become the Lamp of the Eternal unto the world, and His straight, undeviating Path amidst the peoples of the earth. Say: This is the Dayspring of Divine knowledge, if ye be of them that understand, and the Dawning-place of God's commandments, if ye be of those who comprehend.[4] - Bahá'u'lláh

A second source of guidance is the Covenant, which provides authorized interpretation of the Word. The Covenant gives inspiration and knowledge in a way we can all relate to: human lives, faces and voices that nonetheless respond to our deepest needs, protect us from error, serve as a vital link to our Creator, and in other, unseen ways channel spiritual energies into the world of matter.

> Know this for a certainty that today, the penetrative power in the arteries of the world of humanity is the power of the Covenant. The body of the world will not

be moved through any power except through the power of the Covenant. There is no other power like unto this. This Spirit of the Covenant is the real Centre of love and is reflecting its rays to all parts of the globe, which are resuscitating and regenerating man and illuminating the path to the Divine Kingdom.[5] - 'Abdu'l-Bahá

The Divine Kingdom. An elusive dream of mankind for countless generations. Is it really possible, or just a utopia? If anything, a divine kingdom would certainly have to include a whole new paradigm of social order. The existing one is far from paradise. Living in our current paradigm of struggle and oppression, it's hard to even imagine anything else, much less work to achieve it. But if we truly want to loosen the knot of oppression we find ourselves tied up in, we have to have a vision of where we are going. Our guidance must include some idea of the goal.

In 1936 Shoghi Effendi wrote, "The unity of the human race, as envisaged by Bahá'u'lláh, implies the establishment of a world commonwealth in which all nations, races, creeds and classes are closely and permanently united, and in which the autonomy if its state members and the personal freedom and initiative of the individuals that compose them are definitely and completely safeguarded."[6]

He went on to describe this world commonwealth as governed by a world legislature to regulate the use of resources and enact laws, a world executive force to apply the laws and safeguard the unity of the world's peoples, and a world tribunal to settle disputes. Over 70 years ago Shoghi Effendi foresaw the eventual adoption of means and technologies that will bring mankind together into a peaceful, divinely inspired civilization. These include a mechanism for quick, reliable worldwide communication, a large metropolis acting as a nerve center for the world, a universal auxiliary language and script, arts and literature for global audiences, uniform weights and measures, the harmonious coexistence of science and religion, unbiased press and media, and fair distribution of the world's resources. National and racial prejudices and animosities will be resolved, he said, and religious disputes abolished. Large gaps between rich and poor will be closed. Human resources will be diverted from war, and directed towards education, research, health care, and the improvement of life.

Those are some of the material signs of a divine kingdom. It's a vision of a new paradigm, our future civilization free of the knot of oppression. Are you ready for it? Are you ready to help make it happen? Then you're ready to arise for action.

Notes

1. Bahá'u'lláh, *Gleanings from the Writings of Bahá'u'lláh*, LXX
2. Ibid, LXI
3. 'Abdu'l-Bahá, cited in *The World Order of Bahá'u'lláh*, p 169
4. Bahá'u'lláh, *The Kitáb-i-Aqdas*, paragraph 186
5. 'Abdu'l-Bahá, cited in *The Covenant*, number 40
6. Shoghi Effendi, *The World Order of Bahá'u'lláh*, p 203

Getting Started

OK, so now you have the vision. You've seen how the pyramid model of oppression was disrupted by the Báb and Bahá'u'lláh, and how by their inspiration and guidance we can transform ourselves and rebuild society in a whole new way. A complete paradigm shift is now possible, perhaps for the first time in recorded history.

These changes will not come about on their own, though. Action is needed—action from each one of us. But where to start? What to do first?

Here in this final chapter I'm going to share what I think are your best options. These suggestions come from my own experience and personal understanding of Bahá'u'lláh's teachings. They work for me; indeed, they have changed my life. I offer them here for you as practical steps you may wish to take to loosen the knot of oppression in your life.

Recognize

From what I know and have experienced, to truly loosen the knot of oppression, you must strive to recognize the reality of Bahá'u'lláh. Let me explain why.

The deepest form of oppression is oppression of the soul. Ultimately, those who oppress us seek to destroy our spirit, to force us into submission, to completely subjugate our wills. They may use physical torture or mental cruelty to do this. It may happen all at once or over a long period of time, even generations. Oppression this deep touches our very hearts, the core of our being. From what I can see, the most profound way to recover from this kind of oppression is through Divine power.

You see, Bahá'u'lláh teaches that we human beings are both physical beings and spiritual beings. We have been created by an all-knowing and loving Creator, God, to know Him and receive His love. Our hearts were designed by God to be filled with His love. Nothing else can satisfy them. Bahá'u'lláh said, "Thy heart is My home."[1]

Since it is our primary purpose to know and love God, the worst kind of oppression is to be cut off from God and not know how to find Him. This is truly oppression of the soul. Bahá'u'lláh said, "What 'oppression' is more grievous than that a soul seeking the truth, and wishing to attain unto the knowledge of God, should know not where to go for it and from whom to seek it?"[2]

On the other hand, once we have overcome oppression at that level, everything else falls into place. Though we may be locked up in prison, bound to a desk, or slaving away at a fast-food joint, as long as we have the abiding love of God in our hearts, we can be filled with joy. Bahá'u'lláh said, "Armed with the power of Thy name nothing can ever hurt me, and with Thy love in my heart all the world's afflictions can in no wise alarm me."[3]

So the question then becomes, how do we get that way? How do we fill our hearts with that kind of love? How do we come to know God? To know someone we need to see them, to talk with them, to hear their words. How can we know God in that way?

Where is God?

Finding God means different things for different people. Traditionally people have looked to religion for guidance—reading scripture, saying prayers, going to church, synagogue or mosque. Nowadays many believe religion to be at best naive and at worst misleading, misguided or even dangerous. Some have drifted away or given up, while others consider themselves spiritual but not religious. And then there are those who claim that God simply does not exist, or that they just can't know.

I can think of two reasons why God is difficult to find. One reason is that He is silent, invisible, unseen, and undetectable by any human means. We may feel His Presence indirectly in the wonders of nature, the truths of scripture, or the deep silence of meditation, but we cannot know Him in His Essence, as He truly is. How can the created encompass the Creator, after all? What can the painting know of the Painter?

And yet, Bahá'ís believe we can know God—through His Manifestation. This Manifestation appears on earth in the form of a human being who walks with us, talks with us, and guides us. This is the Globe in the pyramid, the divine Messenger who helps us build a relationship with the Creator.

However, because this Messenger seems to be just a normal person, it is not easy to recognize Him. It takes a pure heart. Bahá'u'lláh said, "Never shall mortal eye recognize the everlasting Beauty, nor the lifeless heart delight in aught but in the withered bloom."[4] It's difficult to find something if you don't know what you are looking for, or where to look. And there are many false substitutes. Deceived by physical appearances, pulled this way and that by unfulfilled desires like a bull with a ring in its nose, we become easy targets for anyone wishing to take advantage of us.

This brings us to the second reason for the difficulty in finding God, which is that true religion is often held under lock and key by imposters. They understand the power of the desire that draws us towards God, and have inserted themselves into the equation. They claim to represent God, and thus become the recipients of the devotion of their unsuspecting flocks and congregations. Worse still, some of them take advantage of the name of God and religion for their personal benefit. They become the worst kind of oppressor.

Thankfully, that utter darkness has given way to a new dawn. Bahá'u'lláh, the Manifestation of God for this age, has revealed Himself so clearly that anyone who earnestly seeks Him will find Him. He said, "For whereas in days past every lover besought and searched after his Beloved, it is the Beloved Himself Who now is calling His lovers and is inviting them to attain His presence."[5]

The call has gone out. He has made it clear. We can bypass the clergy altogether. We now have direct access. The presence of Bahá'u'lláh is the presence of God. Recognition of Bahá'u'lláh is recognition of God. He said:

> Naught is seen in My temple but the Temple of God, and in My beauty but His Beauty, and in My being but His Being, and in My self but His Self, and in My movement but His Movement, and in My acquiescence but His Acquiescence, and in My pen but His Pen, the Mighty, the All-Praised. There hath not been in My soul but the Truth, and in Myself naught could be seen but God.[6]

Recognizing Bahá'u'lláh as the Temple of God may not come all at once. For most of us it is a life-long endeavor. In fact, it is difficult to even understand what this kind of recognition means. But it is something worth striving for, because in the striving, we loosen the knot of oppression. Even a glimpse of the reality of Bahá'u'lláh can open us to the path of the true seeker. We long to lay aside all of our earthly attachments to be reunited with the true Beloved.

Reset

To start on the path of recognition we need to reset our lives. As mentioned previously, the key to unlocking our hearts to a fuller understanding and appreciation of Bahá'u'lláh is the Creative Word of God. This Creative Word is readily accessible in the writings of the Báb and Bahá'u'lláh. Bahá'u'lláh said:

> The Word of God may be likened unto a sapling, whose roots have been implanted in the hearts of men. It is incumbent upon you to foster its growth through the living waters of wisdom, of sanctified and holy words, so that its root may become firmly fixed and its branches may spread out as high as the heavens and beyond.[7]

To grow this sapling in our hearts, we start by reading the Word of God. This should be done consistently, every morning and evening. Like rich food, you probably won't be able to take in too much at a time. That's fine, you don't need to read very much to feel the effect. A good place to begin is *The Hidden Words of Bahá'u'lláh*. That's the book I started reading first. Each of its passages are just one or a few sentences, packed with meaning. Any one of them, if you can truly put it into practice, will reset your life in a whole new direction.

As you read the Creative Word, you may find certain phrases that jump out at you, that resonate with you, that seem particularly true or especially dear to you. You may want to keep them with you, to have them handy in your mind and heart, to help you through difficult situations. These are worth memorizing. Sometimes they will stick in your memory, and sometimes you'll have to work at it. Either way, memorizing the Word of God, knowing a passage by heart, will draw you closer to Bahá'u'lláh, closer to God.

Much of the Word of God comes in the form of prayers. Thoughtfully and devotedly reciting these prayers is yet another way to draw closer to God. They help you align your will with God's Will. These are not just any words to repeat mindlessly. They are the words which Bahá'u'lláh Himself has used to address God, a priceless gift that He has shared with us. We can use God's own words to speak to God.

Bahá'u'lláh also encourages us to meditate. We need to think deeply about the meaning of the Creative Word, how it applies to our lives, and how we can put the ideas into action. He did not instruct people in any particular meditation technique, but rather leaves it to each one of us to find what works best for ourselves.

Choice Wine

Reading the Creative Word and memorizing it, along with prayer and meditation, are how we reset ourselves inwardly. How about our outward reality? The reset must take place in our deeds and actions, too. For this Bahá'u'lláh has given us laws—guidance for how to live our lives.

At this point in the conversation I often see the hands fly up. "Oh no," comes the cry, "we are happy being spiritual, but don't tell us what to do." "What about my freedom?" some may ask. "Laws are oppressive," complain others.

Bahá'u'lláh turns that fear completely on its head. His laws do not put us down, they bring us up. He likens them to choice wine. He says, "Think not that We have revealed unto you a mere code of laws. Nay, rather, We have unsealed the choice Wine with the fingers of might and power."[8] To fully reset ourselves on the path towards God, and completely loosen the knot of oppression, we need to live our lives in an entirely new way.

Obedience is a natural outcome of recognition. The two go hand in hand. As we begin to recognize the true reality of Bahá'u'lláh, we instinctively want to follow in His way, to please Him, to do what He would like us to do. As we start to obey the laws, we find ourselves more fully able to recognize Bahá'u'lláh. And with that clearer recognition comes a deeper commitment to obeying the laws.

Enemies to Friends

Our willingness to obey must run very deep, as deep as the place in our hearts where we find the power to turn our enemies into friends. 'Abdu'l-Bahá tells us:

> Bahá'u'lláh has clearly said in His Tablets that if you have an enemy, consider him not as an enemy. Do not simply be long-suffering; nay, rather, love him. Your treatment of him should be that which is becoming

lovers. Do not even say that he is your enemy. Do not see any enemies. Though he be your murderer, see no enemy. Look upon him with the eye of friendship. Be mindful that you do not consider him as an enemy and simply tolerate him, for that is stratagem and hypocrisy. To consider a man your enemy and love him is hypocrisy. This is not becoming of any soul. You must behold him as a friend. You must treat him well. This is right.[9]

It seems utterly impossible—a complete contradiction. How can you not consider someone who hurts or abuses you as your enemy? How can you avoid becoming a hypocrite when you try to love that person?

Bahá'u'lláh tells the story of a young man who had lost his beloved, and was desperately searching for her. Wandering the streets of a city at night, he was seen by a watchman. The watchman got suspicious and started following him. The young man got scared and ran, and so the watchman ran after him. They raced through the city until finally the young man turned down a dead-end street and came to a high wall. In desperation he climbed the wall, and there he found his beloved in a garden. At that moment he cried aloud that the watchman was truly his friend, and he thanked God for sending him.

> Indeed, his words were true; for he had found many a secret justice in this seeming tyranny of the watchman,

and had seen how many a mercy lay hid behind the veil. In one stroke of wrath, the guard had joined one who was athirst in the desert of love to the sea of the beloved, and dispelled the darkness of separation with the shining light of reunion. He had led one who was afar to the garden of nearness, and guided an ailing soul to the heart's physician.[10] - Bahá'u'lláh

The difference in his state of mind before he climbed the wall and after was simply knowledge. His understanding affected how he saw the watchman. Running through the streets, he saw him as his enemy. Later, in the garden, he knew he had really been his friend.

We too have the ability to see the people we think are enemies as our friends. Even when they hurt us, they are actually helping us grow. God has created this world for our benefit, for our spiritual growth. Each of us is growing in some way, and consciously or unconsciously we are helping each other to grow. When someone does something to us that we don't like, we have a choice. We can blame that person for causing us discomfort, and make him our enemy. Or we can understand the situation as an opportunity to build our character, grow closer to God, learn to forgive people, overlook the faults of others, and see that God is working through the misdeeds of that person to somehow bring us closer to Him. In that way we can truly see that person as our friend.

Reflect

You could think of Bahá'u'lláh as a perfect mirror, reflecting the light of God into our lives. In a similar way, when we purify our hearts, we in turn reflect His light to the people and world around us. Reading and memorizing His words, saying His prayers, following His laws, every action in our lives takes on new meaning.

The light we reflect is the light of unity. Bahá'u'lláh's unprecedented revelation opens new vistas of understanding about the Oneness of God, of religion, and of humanity. These start to become expressed in our interactions with people. We no longer draw back or hesitate when we encounter someone from a different social class, race, or religion. We embrace them as brothers and sisters.

Essentially, reflecting the light of God means to re-humanize. We counter the dehumanizing effects of oppression by seeing His light in ourselves and in every other person. We begin to respect each other. Bahá'u'lláh said, "Know ye not why We created you all from the same dust? That no one should exalt himself over the other."[11] We soften our block-like mentality, and begin to see each other as God sees us, as true human beings. Bahá'u'lláh tells us to "be even as one soul, to walk with the same feet, eat with the same mouth and dwell in the same land." [12]

Seeing every person as one of "us" should help ensure the survival of humanity, according to authors Hare and Woods. Turning each one of "them" into one of "us" is the best way to reconcile our instincts for friendliness on one hand and our protective nature on the other. When everyone is part of the same family, there is nobody that you need to defend against. With the danger gone, the mother bear can relax and focus on nurturing her cubs.

Likewise, the care/control duality mentioned by authors Graeber and Wengrow is resolved when we hand over both care and control to God. As we build a deep, trusting relationship with Him, we begin to feel that we—and all with whom we associate—are under His loving care. And as we learn to trust that He will care for our loved ones, we feel less of an urge to control them. This trust can extend beyond our close circle of friends and family, as we become more willing to trust our co-workers, business associates, and even people we pass on the street.

Of course, problems will come up. Differences will arise. They are an inescapable reality of life. Think of them as tests of our growing spiritual capacity. Do we fall into old habits of competition, finding fault, and putting each other down? Or can we change this destructive behavior and truly reflect the light of God? Here is the standard that Bahá'u'lláh sets:

> Conflict and contention are categorically forbidden in His Book.[13]

So simple to say, so easy to memorize, and yet so challenging to do. Imagine going through just one day not arguing with anyone! And now extend that to a week, a year, a lifetime. But it must be possible, because He expects it of us. Difficult as it may seem, when you make a conscious effort to end all conflict, to stop pushing your own ideas, and start to seek resolution and agreement, the whole environment seems to change. You can relax, let go, and let some light into the room —and even into your heart.

In our efforts, we can always turn towards Bahá'u'lláh for help. He said:

> If any differences arise amongst you, behold Me standing before your face, and overlook the faults of one another for My name's sake and as a token of your love for My manifest and resplendent Cause.[14]

One source of conflict in many parts of the world is between political parties. Bahá'u'lláh steers us clear of them so we can freely appreciate good ideas and policies from whatever source they originate. We can vote our conscience, while at the same time look beyond the political system for deeper causes of problems, and possible solutions.

Under Bahá'u'lláh's guidance, our horizons expand. We learn to search out the truth in different areas of life, and begin to value the separate but complementary spheres of science and religion for investigating reality at all levels. We start to view the wonders of creation in a new light, and become more open to the differing viewpoints and opinions of others.

When we truly reflect the light of God, we behold it shining in all things. And this is the secret to loosening the knot of oppression in the world around us. Bahá'u'lláh said:

> We fain would hope that the people of Bahá may be guided by the blessed words: "Say: all things are of God." This exalted utterance is like unto water for quenching the fire of hate and enmity which smoldereth within the hearts and breasts of men. By this single utterance contending peoples and kindreds will attain the light of true unity.[15]

All things are of God. If we make an honest effort to understand what that means, if we keep it in our hearts, bring it to mind, and share it when needed, then we are assured that the fire of hatred and enmity will be quenched, and unity will prevail. This is what it means, to me, to reflect the light of God.

As the light reflects, it spreads out. This joy we feel in our hearts becomes contagious. We are happy to tell others about what we have found. For those who are interested, we share. For those who are not, instead of boring or alienating them, we discuss other things, while continuing to serve them as a friend or well-wisher.

Reach Out

Finally, we are not alone in all this. Others have already found Bahá'u'lláh and are learning to loosen the knot of oppression through His light. Reach out to the Bahá'ís in your area. They will be happy to hear from you. They are living just about everywhere in the world these days—big cities, small towns, and in remote islands and villages. If you don't know where to start, you can go to the website of your national Bahá'í community. These are listed by continent on the Worldwide Bahá'í Community website (www.bahai.org).

The Bahá'ís have a plan for the world, and everyone has a place in it. If there is a Bahá'í community near you, there may be a number of activities you and your friends or family can participate in—devotional meetings, study groups, children's classes, youth activities, and more. The focus is on social transformation and community building. The Universal House of Justice describes it like this:

> The enkindled souls being raised up through the processes of the Plan are seeking to gain an ever more profound understanding of Bahá'u'lláh's teachings —"the sovereign remedy for every disease"—and to apply them to the needs of their society. . . . They advocate tolerance and understanding, and with the inherent oneness of humanity uppermost in their minds, they view everyone as a potential partner to

collaborate with, and they strive to foster fellow feeling even among groups who may traditionally have been hostile to one another.... They see the power that true religion possesses to transform hearts and overcome distrust, and so, with confidence in what the future holds, they labour to cultivate the conditions in which progress can occur.... They share their beliefs liberally with others, remaining respectful of the freedom of conscience of every soul, and they never impose their own standards on anyone. And while they would not pretend to have discovered all the answers, they are clear about what they have learned and what they still need to learn. Their efforts advance to the alternating rhythm of action and reflection; setbacks leave them unfazed.[16]

These are people worth spending time with. Although not every Bahá'í fully embodies this description, most are exerting an honest effort to live up to the high standards that the Universal House of Justice describes. Reach out to them. Join them. Together we may loosen the knot of oppression in this world once and for all.

Of course, we must at all times keep our gaze fixed on the One Who stands before us, the One Who dwells in our hearts, the One Who holds the true power. He tells us:

The friends of God shall win and profit under all conditions, and shall attain true wealth. In fire they remain cold, and from water they emerge dry. Their affairs are at variance with the affairs of men. Gain is their lot, whatever the deal. To this testifieth every wise one with a discerning eye, and every fair-minded one with a hearing ear.[17]

What kind of power is this? This is the kind of power that instilled fear into hearts of the small-minded people who put the Báb and Bahá'u'lláh in prison. This is the power that protected Them and Their followers through all manner of persecution. This is the power that opened the hearts of Bahá'u'lláh's guards, allowing Him to walk freely out of prison. This is the power that toppled kings and despots, and is now breaking down the old world order and rolling out a new one. This is the power that we can reflect, that resets us, that we gain from recognizing Bahá'u'lláh. This is the power that unites us. This is the power that is loosening the knot of oppression.

> Through the movement of Our Pen of glory We have, at the bidding of the omnipotent Ordainer, breathed a new life into every human frame, and instilled into every word a fresh potency. All created things proclaim the evidences of this worldwide regeneration. This is the most great, the most joyful tidings imparted by the Pen of this wronged One to mankind. Wherefore fear ye, O My well-beloved ones? Who is it that can dismay you? A touch of moisture sufficeth to dissolve the hardened

clay out of which this perverse generation is molded. The mere act of your gathering together is enough to scatter the forces of these vain and worthless people.[18]
- Bahá'u'lláh

Notes

1. Bahá'u'lláh, *The Hidden Words of Bahá'u'lláh*, from the Arabic, number 59

2. Ibid, *The Kitáb-i-Íqán*, p 31

3. Ibid, *Prayers and Meditations by Bahá'u'lláh*, CXXII

4. Ibid, *The Hidden Words of Bahá'u'lláh*, from the Persian, number 10

5. Ibid, *Gleanings from the Writings of Bahá'u'lláh*, CLI

6. Ibid, *The Summons of the Lord of Hosts*, paragraph 44

7. Ibid, *Gleanings from the Writings of Bahá'u'lláh*, XLIII

8. Ibid, *The Kitáb-i-Aqdas*, paragraph 5

9. 'Abdu'l-Bahá, *The Promulgation of Universal Peace*, p 267

10. Bahá'u'lláh, *The Call of the Divine Beloved*, The Seven Valleys, paragraph 28

11. Ibid, *The Hidden Words of Bahá'u'lláh*, from the Arabic, number 68

12. Ibid.

13. Bahá'u'lláh, *Tablets of Bahá'u'lláh*, p 22

14. Ibid, *Gleanings from the Writings of Bahá'u'lláh*, CXLVI

15. Ibid, *Tablets of Bahá'u'lláh*, p 222
16. The Universal House of Justice, from a letter to the Conference of the Continental Boards of Counsellors, 30 December 2021.
17. Bahá'u'lláh, cited in *Crisis and Victory*, number 47
18. Ibid, *Tablets of Bahá'u'lláh*, p 84-85

References

'Abdu'l-Bahá. *Memorials of the Faithful*. Wilmette, Bahá'í Publishing Trust, 1971.
———. *Paris Talks*. London, Bahá'í Publishing Trust, 1972.
———. *The Promulgation of Universal Peace*. Wilmette, Bahá'í Publishing Trust, 1982.
———. *Selections from the Writings of 'Abdu'l-Bahá*. Haifa, Bahá'í World Centre, 1978.
———. *Some Answered Questions*. Haifa, Bahá'í World Centre, 2014.
———. *Tablets of the Divine Plan*. Wilmette, Bahá'í Publishing Trust, 1977.
———. *Will and Testament of 'Abdu'l-Bahá*. Wilmette, Bahá'í Publishing Trust, 1971.
Báb, The. *Selections from the Writings of the Báb*. Haifa, Bahá'í World Centre, 1976.
Bahá'í International Community. *The Prosperity of Humankind*. New York, 1995.
Bahá'í Prayers. Wilmette, Bahá'í Publishing Trust, 1982.
Bahá'u'lláh. *The Call of the Divine Beloved*. Haifa, Bahá'í World Centre, 2018.
———. *Epistle to the Son of the Wolf*. Wilmette, Bahá'í Publishing Trust, 1979.

———. *Gleanings from the Writings of Bahá'u'lláh*. Wilmette, Bahá'í Publishing Trust, 1976.

———. *The Hidden Words of Bahá'u'lláh*. Wilmette, Bahá'í Publishing Trust, 1975.

———. *Kitáb-i-Aqdas (The Most Holy Book)*. Haifa, Bahá'í World Centre, 1992.

———. *Kitáb-i-Íqán (The Book of Certitude)*. Wilmette, Bahá'í Publishing Trust, 1974.

———. *Prayers and Meditations*. Wilmette, Bahá'í Publishing Trust, 1979.

———. *The Summons of the Lord of Hosts*. Haifa, Bahá'í World Centre, 2002.

———. *Tablets of Bahá'u'lláh Revealed after the Kitáb-i-Aqdas*. Haifa, Bahá'í World Centre, 1978.

Zinn, Howard. *A People's History of the United States*. New York, HarperCollins, 1995.

Effendi, Shoghi. *God Passes By*. Wilmette, Bahá'í Publishing Trust, 1974.

———. *The World Order of Bahá'u'lláh*. Wilmette, Bahá'í Publishing Trust, 1980.

Freire, Paulo. *Pedagogy of the Oppressed*. New York, The Continuum Publishing Company, 1993.

Graeber, David and Wengrow, David. *The Dawn of Everything: A New History of Humanity*. Canada, Penguin Random House, 2022.

References

Hare, Brian and Woods, Vanessa. *Survival of the Friendliest: Understanding Our Origins and Rediscovering Our Common Humanity*. New York, Random House, 2022.

Nabíl-i-A'zam. *The Dawn Breakers*. Wilmette, Bahá'í Publishing Trust, 1932.

Universal House of Justice. Letter to the Conference of the Continental Boards of Counsellors. Haifa, Bahá'í World Centre, 30 December 2021.

Universal House of Justice Research Department. *Consultation: A Compilation*. Haifa, Bahá'í World Centre, 1990.

———. *Crisis and Victory*. Haifa, Bahá'í World Centre, 1987.

———. *The Covenant*. Haifa, Bahá'í World Centre, 1987.